"We first met Jay when I was West End. She sent a letter to showed it to my wife, Donna, bubbly Jay came to the show with were able to hang out a little while seemed even more serendipitous when I learned her story. She and her cousin, Sandy, had been lifelong Monkees fans! Jay's writing is inspired…We feel she will soon move beyond her small town in Wales to a more global platform. She is truly a gifted communicator!" **Micky and Donna Dolenz** – The Monkees

"Sensitive and beautifully written, Jay absorbs you into her world and shares love, laughter and tears. You will find a new friend here." **India Redman** – Artist & Writer, Cloudhorse Design, NM, USA

"This is such a poignant story from which a flame of love burns eternal." **Jackie Weaver** – Author of *Changing Lives*

"This book brings back so many happy memories for me…of my home town and my youth, but mainly of my friendship with one of life's special people, Sandy. She had a beauty that many people could never see, or didn't take the time to discover, and she will always be in my heart." **Michael Dore** – Singer: www.michaeldore.com

"Reading Jay's book very much took me back to my days as a child and her style of writing was reminiscent of that of Enid Blyton. Her way of writing brought back the child in me. Yet interwoven within her simple way of relating her story was the more innate and profound message about that of a deep friendship, a love woven between two women not just on the physical plane, but one which carried on into the non-physical plane, a spiritual plane of for-everness. Jay's honest and sincere portrayal of her feelings of loss and love is a great reminder of what should be important in our lives. This book added dimensions to my understanding of love and encapsulated extremely well the reality of unconditional love and how this influences and affects our lives and who we are and the extraordinary bond between two people that can last for a lifetime." **Esther Austin** – Radio Presenter, Author, Spiritual Healer

"A beautiful and heartfelt story that lovingly reminds us that there really is no death; that we are eternal and that aspects of the non-physical are always communicating with us. Jay's experiences, which she so authentically shares with us, will put a smile on your face as it did mine." **Sierra Goodman** – Radio Presenter, Photographer and President of Vida Marina Dolphin Conservation, Costa Rica: www.vidamarina.org

"There are millions of children around the world suffering with unrepaired clefts - Smile Train is delighted that through the publication of this book many more will receive the free surgery they so desperately need, giving them a new smile and a second chance at life." **Meg Flanagan** – Smile Train: www.smiletrain.org

"This is a very moving story that enthrals but evokes deep fears, prejudices and issues all humans feel difficult to deal with but the enduring message is that true love overcomes everything life can throw at us." **Stephanie Booth** – Businesswoman, Star of BBC's *Hotel Stephanie* and Author of *A Girl in a Million*

"A Work of Heart is an amazing story of recognizing and engaging with love through all time and space. Jay has taken us on her story of remembering the infinite connection we have with others, no matter where they are. As one reads this amazing story, one remembers at a very deep level our ability to stay connected, whether someone is still with us here in physical or have moved on to non-physical time-space. Love is truly timeless and transcendent of all time and space. Jay's connection with Sandra and their amazing stories warm the heart and help connect each of us to those we love." **Shelle Pourmanafzadehardabili** – Corporate Director of Marketing, Rock Resorts and Vail Resorts Hospitality

*To dear Uncle Gord & Auntie Joan,*
*with love from the Heart*
*Jillie (JAY!) and Sandy*
*x xx*
*x*

# A Work of Heart –
# Eagles, Deserts, Monkees and Canyons

*The story of an extraordinary friendship that
transcended space, time and physical death.*

Jay Atkinson

Local Legend Publishing UK

ISBN 978-1-907203-15-2

Local Legend Publishing 2010
Park Issa
St Martin's Road
Gobowen, Shropshire
SY11 3NP, UK
www.local-legend.co.uk

Cover Design by Titanium Design
www.titaniumdesign.co.uk

Cover illustration © iStockphoto.com/TommL
Internal photographic images © Jay Atkinson
All rights reserved

The names of individuals in this book have been changed, where applicable, to protect people's privacy

To my beautiful Sandy – Take it Easy 'til we meet again…

# *Acknowledgements*

Kim, my darling husband. Truly the string on the end of my kite! The Bert to my Mary Poppins. For your love, your patience, your kindness, your tolerance and your support – I adore you.

Dawn Lewis for her unsurpassed and unwavering faith in my *scribblings* ever since I met her in 1974. She encouraged and endorsed every word ever I wrote and never doubted that this book would be born, even when I doubted myself. Thank you from my heart and soul, dear lady. I love you.

Paul M – you know who you are! For being there to catch the angel who had lost her wings, my eternal appreciation. Without your validation, this book would never have been given the breath of life.

Anna, Jamie and Kate. No words can express how much I love these three wonderful people. My kids…

Beth – Publisher of this work of heart. Beautiful Beth, without whom none of this would have been possible. Thank you from Sandy and me for giving unconditional love and life to our dream.

The late, great John Denver – another magical instrument through which Sandy Miracles manifested over time. When his beautiful song, *Sunshine on my Shoulder* manifested itself one day in a 1970's film of the same name, it broke my heart. The film is about the death of a young woman who leaves behind a baby son and his father and is beautiful and sad and happy at the same time. A few weeks later this lovely song burst into life again on my radio, accompanied a rainbow in the sky and a butterfly on my shoulder on a 'missing Sandy' day, my heart filled with sunshine and my soul soared, as it does with all of his music. Thank you JD – I now know you are Everywhere…

My lovely friends and family without whom this life experience would be hollow and meaningless. Each and every one of you is precious to me. Whether or not you are still in my life, I appreciate your contribution to it. I love you.

Solomon – the beautiful 12ft owl who showed up at the foot of my bed to give wings to my process. Your wisdom is eternal, as is your presence.

# Contents

# *Foreword*

This book has been written with all of my heart and soul. It is intended that my experience be shared with as many people as possible, because as the old saying goes, 'Two things are certain in this world: death and taxes!' At some stage in everyone's life, they will encounter death. Everyone has a different experience and there is no time limit on grieving. I don't need to write *War and Peace* all over again to give you the picture. So this is not a lengthy tome. But I do hope that it will bring upliftment to your heart, in the knowledge that you cannot die for the life of you and we do go on, albeit in the energetic sense, not the physical. If this book serves only to provide a bridge across forever, my experience will have been validated for me and for Sandy.

Sandy was my cousin and my friend but more importantly she was a part of me. When she died in 1997 aged 41, I wanted to die with her. My grief blinded me to all goodness, until I realised that Sandy was still around. Evidence of her showed up all around me in ways I found at first difficult to comprehend, but as time progressed, I realised she hadn't really gone anywhere. Her physicality had ceased to be, but the true inner being of my beloved friend and life companion had remained. In fact, not only had her energy self remained but her personality was expanding beyond where she had evolved whilst in the physical. The accounts I share with you here are the facts as they happened to me. I know Sandy is still here and every day more evidence appears that our work together continues.

I have learned through speaking to other people, that it is generally uncommon to have a friendship that lasts a lifetime, let alone one that survives the death experience! Most people have friends and many have long-term friendships, but the ones that weather all storms from beginning to end are rarer. Friendships are very transient, especially in our day and age where people up sticks and travel around the globe. In the 1950's it was perhaps a less itinerant population due to lack of funds and lack of transport! I feel it important to let my readers know some of the background to my amazing relationship with Sandy and so it is written in distinct parts. The first part is the 'getting to know you' part; this covers childhood into adulthood and conveys some of the experiences we shared that made our friendship solid and unique. The second part is about Sandy's untimely death and my subsequent withdrawal from the world at large. I found the grief unbearable at times and just wanted to be with her, wherever she was. The third part is still a work in progress… she showed me, quite simply, that you can't die for the life of you! After her transition, which I prefer to call it nowadays, Sandy very quickly became my 'guide', unseen companion and mentor, through dreams and other miracle happenings. We have continued growing together – she from the other world and me from down here on Earth. She can still make me lose control of my bladder with laughter!

You may be wondering about the title of the book and how it came to be. The original write up of what has evolved into the current version, was truly a Work of Heart, and that is what I was going to call it. However, some years down the line and with new perspectives, I decided to re-write what had mainly been my catharsis, my healing, into a joyful story. Writing, it turned out, was the only way I could get through the pain and it somehow made Sandy more valid. When someone you love dies, a light goes out in your life. Your soul can feel as if it has had a part of it torn away and lost. If the loved one has been cremated and the ashes spirited away by one of the family, as happened in my case, there will be no physical or geographical place you can take your grief. It begins to feel as if they never existed or that you must be going mad. I desperately needed to feel that Sandy's life had not been in vain. Nor mine come to that.

I know that someday Sandy and I will join hands again and Jive our way through the heavens, wearing only our angel wings and a smile.

Until that day, I have to be content with her unseen presence. She is the 'absent friend' I toast every morning and evening and Christmas and birthday. Her presence is my gift.

She was and continues to be the *Wind beneath my Wings…*

# Part 1

# *In the Beginning*

My first encounter with a funny little kid they called my cousin, was in my granny's back yard. It was a hot summer day in July 1959; the kind of day that made you wish you had a swimming pool. Three friends were playing contentedly on the picnic rug (an old flannelette sheet that my granny had grown weary of patching up) on the six square feet of grass that granny called her garden, and were happily doling out watery tea and crab paste sandwiches from the dinky china tea set that I'd been given for my birthday in April.

Debra and Penelope (Debbie and Penny) lived next door and the wall between the two pre-war terraced houses had been demolished due to age and disrepair, and for a time, our worlds merged and we could move freely between the two houses. No barriers. Kid's paradise. Debbie was a year younger than me, and her sister, Penny, was a couple of years older. Debbie was my best friend and we shared everything. We would have been about three years old and Penny would have been five or six.

This lovely buzzy-bee, lazy day was soon to be shattered by the arrival of 'Our Sandra'. She was my Aunty Joyce's younger daughter and, until that day, I had been unaware of her presence. Aunty Joyce was my mum's maternal cousin and she and Uncle Ted lived a few streets away in Wellington Street, Grimsby. They had two daughters, Sandra and an older daughter. Sandra's sister was very pretty.

Every Friday in Grimsby was 'Market Day' and after a frenzied shop for the weekly groceries in the cobbled, covered market in Freeman Street – main shopping area for the locals of the town – all the ladies would congregate for a welcome cup of tea and a gossip, usually at my granny's house. The children, naturally, were dispatched outside to play.

Sandra appeared from nowhere and stood defiantly at the edge of the circle of friends. She wanted to muscle in on our game and we were having none of it. In any case, there were no sandwiches left and the 'tea' in the pot had been drained. I told this strange little child to go away, and she did, only to return two minutes later with a packet of Daz from her mother's shopping bag, which she had somehow managed to prise open in order to dump it all over my head!

There was a lot of caterwauling and dramatics on my behalf, being a theatrical and highly vocal drama queen, and as I struggled for breath trying to avoid choking on the soapy dusty stuff, Sandra was hauled inside for a telling off and a good smack. Justice had been done and as granny cleaned me up, I was pacified with a bag of dolly mixtures, which always worked with me.

It was only later that I realised Sandra didn't look the same as us. She was a funny looking little kid, and I thought she looked a bit like my teddy bear. This was on account of her having been born with a cleft palate, a hare lip and a 'wry neck' – which basically meant that her head was sitting squarely on her shoulders without the benefit of a neck. She looked as if she had been fashioned out of plasticine and had somehow melted. This is not meant to be an unkind description of my lovely girl, but as children, we view things a little differently from adults and also we are not judgemental; more observational and honest about our observations.

I later learned from my mum that as I had been born in April of 1956, Aunty Joyce gave birth to her little bundle six weeks later at the end of May. Sandra Coulbeck stormed into the world with impact. It was recalled by my mother, some years later, that Aunty Joyce's screams could be heard streets away, when her bundle of joy was born with a huge hole in her face and two large balls of flesh stuck to the side of her head that should have been a nose and mouth.

One can only imagine the distress of a mother who had already given birth to a perfect and very pretty girl child, and who found herself in a minority. In those days, things weren't as accepted as maybe they are now and medical help was very rudimentary, especially when it came to reconstructive or plastic surgery. Aunty Joyce and Uncle Ted took it in turns, around the clock, to feed the tiny and helpless infant with a dropper. She had no means of sucking a bottle teat, and so the only way to get milk into her was to painstakingly drip it into the opening on her face, drop by drop. The years that followed were a round of over 15 different operations to make Sandra appear 'normal'. Uncle Ted adored his little girl and love and attention were heaped upon her, sadly to the detriment of his other lovely girl. He wanted to protect his child, understandably, from the harsh and cruel realities of life.

As life unfolded, Sandra and I learned more about one another and as we were family, we were thrown together quite a lot, through family 'hatches, matches and dispatches', as my granny called them, and soon realised we shared a great deal in common. Her mother would often hand me down her clothes because Sandra was bigger than me. I was a very small child for my age and Sandra grew rapidly as her mum shovelled good home cooking down her neck in order to 'build her up'. I think, looking back, Aunty Joyce was subconsciously trying to shield her little girl from the life she knew lay before her. I was particularly fond of Sandra's swanky red anorak. They were the fashion item to be seen with when I was five years old, and my mum couldn't afford one, so when Sandra outgrew hers and it was passed to me, I was delighted.

Children can be unbearably cruel and it was not long before it was time to go to school and face some of those harsh realities we were thus far protected from. Sandra and I attended the same school for a while, as it was in close proximity to both our homes. That is where our friendship was cemented and later we went to Brownies and Girl Guides together and formed an alliance that was to last a lifetime… and beyond. I was even given Sandra's cast off Girl Guide uniform when we went to our first Guide Camp aged 11. That was a hoot. The Cherry Garth Girl Guide and Boy Scout camp was in Humberston. Humberston was the posh part of Cleethorpes, where the affluent businessmen and retired skippers lived in palatial dream houses, with sweeping driveways. The country lanes were lined with mature and beautiful trees. Cherry Garth was a huge field somewhere in the midst of all this splendour and was surrounded by woodland. It was given over to the Scouts and Guides as a jamboree venue.

We were away from home for a week and, after two days, most of the girls had cried themselves to sleep at least once, with homesickness. Good grief… home was only about two miles away, but you would have thought we were in the outback. Sandra and I relished the Sunday visit from the relatives and were delighted when our grannies turned up in the back of Uncle Ted's Ford Anglia with bags full of goodies and lemonade. My mum and dad didn't come.

They were too busy nursing their hangovers to have the energy to come and see their child!

During the week, it rained incessantly and everything we owned got soaked. The tent leaked and our sleeping bags were soggy, but we were determined to stick it out. The one day we got sunshine, we were off into the woods to find green sticks to whittle, so that we could make doughy balls of fire-bread to toast over the campfire. My stick was so green it still had leaves on it, but they made the dough-balls taste better. That night, Sandra was sick, which set up a chain reaction of heaving in the next tent. It was chaos, but good old Brown Owl and Akela dealt with the fallout admirably. We did learn, however, to wash our clothes and peg them out on the guy ropes. Sandra and I shared a tent with her sister and her friend, Polly, so they at least took care of us, soothing us with tales from the crypt and scaring us sleepless every night. Was I ever glad to go home to a hot bath and a palatable meal!

There were many occasions when some of the children who didn't know Sandra first saw her, would either run away crying, or shout and call her names. It is remarkable how, when we are frightened of something or don't understand it, we react with fear and in defence.

Every time something bad happened to Sandra, I seemed to be in close proximity, and like a Tasmanian devil, I would launch a physical and verbal attack upon anyone who upset her. All I could see and hear were their words and actions that hurt her feelings badly and rather than defend herself, she would take herself off into a little corner and try to be invisible. For someone I knew as having a personality larger than life and who had the most wonderful sense of humour, it was hard for me to take and I wasn't going to see my cousin and friend battered like that.

And so, enter stage right, Sandra Coulbeck after which my life would never be the same. I am happy that she was in my life for a brief period and I know that when I return to the Source she will be the first to greet me. Can't wait!

# *Beauty is only skin deep… Ugly runs all the way through!*

The following anecdotes serve to give but a glimpse of the funny, sad, wonderful rollercoaster ride that formed our friendship. I can feel everything happening over again as I write and am so grateful for the experience of life that we shared.

An event springs to mind of one summer evening in August when Sandy and I had a night out planned. She and I loved dressing up and going dancing and we didn't do it often, but this night was special, as it was a Motown tribute band called The Rumble Band. They had been playing in and around the town for many years and were very good, and as Sandy and I loved Motown music, I bought two tickets as a surprise belated birthday gift to her. We headed into Cleethorpes, which as a seaside resort had, at the time, seen better days but which was in the middle of being re-marketed and 'tarted up' (an Aunt Joyce-ism). The concert began at 8pm at the Winter Gardens. Every seaside resort has to have a Winter Gardens, doesn't it? I hear it is no longer there, due to lack of financial support and the need to redevelop the land into boxes called property. Anyway, prior to going to the Winter Gardens, we decided to visit one of the bars on the seafront for a couple of glasses of wine to get the good vibrations flowing! Standing at the bar were four very drunken males, who were leering at anything in a skirt, nay, with two legs. Sandy waited politely (she was always getting told off by me for being too polite at times) for the barman to take our order and I went to find us a seat.

As she walked towards me with the glasses of wine, I could see that she was shaking and she looked pale and upset. "Are you okay, sweets?" I asked her. She didn't like to make a fuss and so she tried to cover up her emotions but I persisted. My Tasmanian devil radar was off the scale and I just knew it had something to do with the yobs at the bar. After some prompting, she told me that one of them had turned to her and asked, "Don't I recognise you from somewhere?"

To which she had replied, politely, "I don't think so, I might have remembered." This was her naïve attempt at batting back what she thought could be a compliment.

"Oh, I think I do," he continued, "at the zoo… in the Monkey House. That's what you f***ing look like, love." He then laughed in her face and watched her embarrassment, as she turned away, mortified and humiliated.

On hearing this, my blood boiled and I was not about to let this lout spoil her evening or mine. I calmly walked to the bar and ordered the biggest glass of red wine they had and took it back to the table. "What's that for?" asked Sandy.

"You'll see," said I.

We chatted a little more until it was time to leave for the concert and I pushed her in front of me toward the door. As I passed the moron who had offended my girl, I calmly tipped the full glass of red wine over his head, and down his new, white and expensive shirt. His mates all gasped, and backed away, as their friend spluttered and coughed and looked bewildered.

"Oy! You! Beauty is only skin deep, but remember - ugly runs ALL the way through, buster. And you have ugly stamped all the way through you like the letters in a stick of Cleethorpes Rock," I hissed into his stupid face. Then, to Sandy, "Quick, run like the bloody clappers," which we did. We laughed so much that we tripped up on the Winter Gardens' steps and made a rather undignified entrance, but we didn't give two hoots. We danced like we hadn't danced in years and the evening ended in triumph! Revenge is a dish best served cold? Nah! Revenge, on this occasion, was a dish best served in a wine glass!

## *Telepathy or Coincidence?*

Sandy and I attended Holme Hill Junior School together. She lived across the road from the school and I lived a short walk away. Our class teacher was a very ancient spinster named Miss Schofield, who had huge bosoms that were tightly bound in a Victorian contraption that was obviously very uncomfortable for her. Unfortunately for her, she also wore a very ill-fitting wig. The class found it hilarious to watch this wayward hairpiece, nicknamed 'Wiggy', moving around, as if it had a life of its own. I'm sure we were collectively willing it to fall off. Wicked children! She had a foul temper when crossed and it was all we could do sometimes not to call out, "Keep yer wig on Miss." This would have been all the encouragement she needed to come and haul you up onto your desk and give your ankles a good slapping. Nowadays, we could have sued her for damages!

One day, Miss Schofield set us a task to write a story. She chalked up six subject choices upon the blackboard and each of us were to pick a title and write a story about it. A few days after we'd completed this task and handed in our papers, Miss Schofield called Sandra and me out to the front of the class. Although my mother would have bet her five-inch Italian stiletto heeled shoes to the contrary, I was extremely shy, especially under scrutiny, and so was Sandra. We stood at the front of the class together, shuffling our feet, painfully conscious of being centre stage. Miss Schofield asked if we were aware that we had chosen the same title for our stories. We shook our heads, murmuring, "No, Miss Schofield," anxious to be out of the limelight, but our teacher eyed us suspiciously and asked more questions. It appeared that not only had we chosen the same story title, we had virtually written the same story! The poor old dear adjusted her bosoms and it was obvious that she was trying to buy herself some time. She simply didn't believe that we had not collaborated in some way, and remained in a state of awe for the rest of the lesson. I think we had unnerved her because she kept readjusting 'Wiggy' and each time she did, the errant hairpiece looked more ruffled. For the remaining period of time that we were her pupils, she viewed us as strange and I suspect she was rather glad when we moved onward and upward!

This was one example of how close Sandra and I were. Over time, we realised we had a telepathic empathy with one another. Many times we would say the same thing at the same time, or have the same idea and always she could reduce me to tears of laughter with one look that spoke a thousand words – words that only she and I knew the meaning of. It really felt as if we were one body, mind and spirit at times and it was spooky.

# Jay Atkinson

## *Uncle Ted and Aunt Joyce*

Growing up was a mixture of things for both of us. Her mum and dad were quite strict parents and mine were quite the opposite. When we were older, we would fall about laughing as she did a chilling impersonation of her mother's shrill call when it was time to go home to tea and bed. Aunty Joyce was quite formidable, and I grew up believing that she didn't like me very much. I think it was my mother she disapproved of more, because my mother was a 'flighty piece' according to Aunty Joyce. Mum had been divorced from my father, when I was not much more than a year old, and we had moved back to live with her mother and father in a two-up, two-down terraced house in Fraser Street, Grimsby. Mum had to go out to work to support us, and so granny raised me.

Sandra's mum and dad were like Darby and Joan. They were a solid couple that worked as a team for their home and family. Uncle Ted owned the small but prestigious Lion Garage, a small business where he repaired the cars of everyone in the town, it seemed. Aunty Joyce was a housewife and mother who took care of the home and family, much as a Sergeant Major might take care of his troops in the barracks! Aunty Joyce scared me a little, but Uncle Ted was a great big handsome chap, who had been in the Merchant Navy and had travelled all over the world during wartime. 'Our Ted' as he was known in the family, was 'as soft as grease', according to my granny, and wouldn't harm a fly, although if his loved ones were under threat, he would transform 'like Jekyll and Hyde'! Sandy and I found it highly comical that our family had these amusing descriptive phrases for every occasion that made no sense to anyone else.

## *You can take the girl out of Grimsby...*

As time went on, many of the people in the terraced streets moved up in the world and relocated to the posh houses on the outskirts of the town. Many of the houses nearby had been bombed during the war and were still in a state of dilapidation or had been condemned. Our street was only a 15 minute walk away from the dockside; Grimsby and Cleethorpes being situated on the North East coast of

England. It was a prime target for the Hun, as the oldies recalled. Most of the kids down our street would play on the 'bomb buildings', in spite of the inherent dangers. I don't recall many of us falling prey to the broken masonry and jagged metal – it was great fun to build a shelter out of old bricks and rubble and play 'house' with your friends.

Grimsby, a busy and thriving fishing port, was home to many fishing families. Some of the trawlermen were deckhands or cooks and some were skippers. There was a lot of jealousy and rivalry between families due to the fact that skippers got the lion's share of the catch financially, so were able to afford to live in the best houses in the nicer parts of town and suburbs. Most had flashy cars and at least one, to my knowledge, had a Rolls Royce. The wives of these men were always well heeled and usually flashing a ton of gold jewellery (albeit vulgar) and this made the other wives envious. Fishing was Grimsby's main industry, so at least everyone maintained a healthy diet that included a shoal of fresh fish for tea at least once a week.

Sometimes after a hearty tea, consisting of bread and jam, 'chucky eggs and soldiers' or spaghetti on toast with lashings of hot, sweet tea, we would go outside to play. The girls would skip in the middle of the road, with a huge length of someone's discarded washing line and the boys would compete for marbles along the gutters. Occasionally, we dared one another to play kiss-chase, which involved the girls screaming theatrically, as the boys chased us and tried to kiss us. Of course, some of us developed an inability to run very fast and this resulted in a few awkward teeth-clashing moments, albeit of pure pleasure!

As dusk fell, some of the older kids would be given a few coppers to go to the 'chippie' for four pennorth of chips. My granddad would send me and Debbie to the fish shop for a 'piece and six', which roughly translated was a piece of haddock the size of a small whale, and six pennorth of chips, wrapped in newspaper and drenched in salt and vinegar. The vinegar was so strong, it would bring tears to your eyes, but it was the tastiest vinegar in the world and you couldn't eat chips without it. Our treat was to have six pennorth of chips between us. Luxury!

Sandra was not allowed to play out much after 6:30pm because she had school the next day. Her mum and dad ran a tight ship and both girls were fed, scrubbed and up the wooden hill to Bedfordshire as the strains of Coronation Street were dying out on the black and white telly.

# Gran's and Nana's

Sandra's nana was my gran's older sister. There were about ten sisters in the family and all of them, at one time or another, lived in the same street. Many of them had married from their family home, in the same street, and didn't travel further than Cleethorpes, except for our Aunty Nora, who had allegedly run away from home and married a man she met at Nottingham Goose Fair. Aunty Doll said they all went on a charabanc one day to this famous fair and Aunty Nora never came back! I don't know if this was a slight exaggeration, but I will grant her poetic licence on this one, as I have no way of checking the authenticity of the story.

Aunty Doll was a lovely nana and was also Aunty Joyce's mum and my granny's sister. Aunty Doll was soft and caring, whereas my granny could be quite hard-faced (Aunty Doll's description, not mine). I think Aunty Joyce should have been my granny's daughter, as they were quite similar in disposition; sticklers for white tea towels and Betterwear Beeswax Furniture Polish, and quite Victorian when it came to the business of raising children.

"Children should be seen and not heard," was the war cry, whenever Sandra or I attempted to join in a conversation that was, quite clearly, only meant for the grown-ups. With one raise of her dreaded eyebrow, Aunty Joyce could have dispatched a fleet of marines without so much as a word being spoken. Sandra and I grew to be very wary of that eyebrow.

Both of us loved our grandmothers passionately. When the mums said, "No', the grannies said, "Okay," and we were a little bit spoiled by them. At any opportunity we would sleep over at granny's house. Aunty Doll lived three doors away at No. 47 and my granny lived at No. 53. When we moved to the 'posh houses' which were two bus rides away, we would convene a secret meeting, engineered with precision so that her mum would allow her to stay at her nana's and mine would allow me to as well. That way, we could get up to mischief *and* be spoiled to death. Sandra's mum wouldn't allow her to have sweets, or 'clarts' as she called them. My mum wasn't fussed and so I had an ample supply, which Sandra and I shared greedily whenever we got chance. One of our favourite sweet shops, Lisles, sold home-made ice lollies that Mrs Lisles made in old cracked china cups. She would make up a batch of fruit squash and stick a wooden lolly stick into the liquid and then freeze them in her big old chest freezer at the back of the shop. They cost threepence each, we're talking old money here, and were a real treat. One afternoon, after we'd whinged and whined and conned our grannies into giving us threepence each, we ran to Lisles's and bought a lolly each. We were well into the frozen confections when suddenly we heard the inimitable cry of Aunty Joyce calling out... "SAN-DRAAAAA." She would call out SANDRA in two parts and tones, starting in a low tone rising to a high pitched semi-scream... 'San----draaa', with emphasis on the 'draaaa'. To this day, I can hear it in my mind and freeze like a rabbit in the headlights.

Sandra stuffed the gigantic lolly into her mouth and ran like the clappers into the alleyway and was promptly sick all over her new, white plimsolls. When Aunty Joyce caught up with her and found out about the lolly, not only did Sandra get a good hiding, but she was banned from seeing me for a week on account of me being a 'bad influence', and woe betide her if she set foot in Lisles's shop again. I think even poor Mrs Lisles got a tongue lashing from Aunty Joyce for allowing Sandra to spend a precious threepence on 'clarts'... it was some time before we dared do that again and even longer before we dared set foot in the shop.

## *Growing Up*

As we grew older, it was obvious that boys were going to be part of the picture at some stage. Sandra had many unrequited crushes during our schooldays. Her mother always put paid to any shenanigans, and we were warned not to go 'ladding it' when we were finally declared old enough to attend the Saturday matinee at the local ABC cinema. Sandra had a crush on Graham, a handsome Cliff Richard lookalike. He was only about ten years old, but his mother parted and slicked down his dark hair with his father's Brylcreem, and despite the fact that you could smell him a mile off, all the girls in our class thought he was a dreamboat! I secretly liked him too, but I had a code of conduct where Sandra was concerned, because although I didn't realise it then, I grew up to feel that I somehow had an unfair advantage in that I was quite pretty, and I felt ashamed of the fact.

My mother would dress me in frothy, girly dresses and tie my hair up in white ribbons, whereas Sandra's mum favoured a parsimonious approach to fashion. The girls always wore rather clumpy, heavy duty, sensible shoes and utility frocks topped with home knit cardies. Aunty Joyce had no time for fripperies, and having grown up in wartime, she was thrifty to the point of stinginess. I was allowed to have long hair, which my mother, a closet hairdresser, would fashion in plaits, ringlets and all sorts of ridiculous hair-dos. I think she was using me as her Girls World mannequin, because she was never allowed to have long hair, due to fear of nits. Go figure that one out. It made me sad to discover that my mum had desperately wanted to be a hairdresser when she left school at the tender age of 14, but my granddad said NO on account that they couldn't afford for her to go on to further education or apprenticeship, so she had to go into the job he had lined up for her in the bird seed factory at the back of our house. Mum said she finished school on the Friday and on the Monday she was marched off to the factory. Poor Mum.

Aunty Joyce, on the other hand, had a mane of beautiful, thick curls, which she wore in Marcel waves. During wartime, she wore her hair in a turban or scarf, as did many women. They all fancied themselves as Dorothy Lamour or Lana Turner, it seems, and the most commonly worn hairstyle was with a side parting and the sides rolled up into Kirby grips. Vanity was not something that was widely encouraged by the mothers of 'nice gels', but was something that was inescapable when hormones started raging, the Yanks were in town, and cosmetics and clothing were scarce. To this day, I can hear Uncle Ted berating our over-the-pond neighbours for being, "Over paid, over sexed and bloody well over here." I don't think he ever got over Aunt Joyce's crush on a G.I. while he was away in the Merchant Navy.

Consequently, Aunty Joyce's approach to clothing her children was somewhat spartan. Her daughters always had warm clothing on, but it was usually lacking in feminine allure and very unflattering. For instance, Sand was forced to wear a ridiculous Pixie hat to school – headgear worn by many young girls of school age as it was the easiest thing for their mothers to knit... Sand just looked like a Cabbage Patch Kid in hers, bless her, and she hated it!

By the time we had hit our teens, my mum had married my step-dad and we had moved out to a 'posh house' in the suburbs. When we first moved into what seemed like rather a palatial semi, we thought we'd died and gone to Hollywood. We had a 'through lounge', for heaven's sake! We had a drive (swoon), a front and back garden (breathless now), and my mother had her first ever bathroom (lie down and take a powder). We thought we had struck oil... not so far removed from the Clampetts after all. And if you're reading this and are under 50, you won't remember the Clampetts. Be grateful for that.

Uncle Ted had a very successful albeit small garage business, although he played his success down modestly for years until he died. He would always plead poverty and after Sandy inherited his stash, we discovered the many ways in which his thrift had been utilised. Sandy took me upstairs to their bathroom one time and pointed at the shower. "What?" I asked. "What am I looking at here?"

"My bloody dad, the skinflint. Look – when the turning knob thingy for the shower broke he refused to buy another one, telling me and Mum that he couldn't afford it. So the old bugger screwed on a Nescafe coffee lid and made do. We've been putting up with that for six years. On Monday, I'm having the whole bathroom ripped out and a new shower put in. That will show him!" and having said that, she stomped off down to make us some tea.

Uncle Ted's thrift over the years meant they moved into a four-bedroom house around the corner from us. I loved their house. It was still a semi, but it was much bigger than our house and they had the luxury of central heating. My dad wouldn't have central heating as he said it 'made you soft'... truth was, he couldn't afford it and was just a little bit envious of Uncle Ted's autonomous income, I believe.

On Saturday nights, the parents went 'up the Mess'. The Mess was an evening venue at the local airfield in Binbrook. During wartime, Lincolnshire was littered with airfields and aerodromes, so we were very familiar with planes of all shapes and sizes. Sometimes, the famous Red Arrows, who left us breathless with their precision aerobatic skills, treated us to an impromptu display.

My dad always seemed envious of Uncle Ted. For one thing he was very handsome and my mum fancied him and secondly, Uncle Ted knew people (tap side of nose for theatrical effect). He was 'in' with the local police force because he repaired all their cars, and he was 'in' with the RAF lads at Binbrook, because of 'other', more clandestine connections. Dad said it couldn't have been from his wartime antics, because the RAF didn't mix with the Merchant Navy, but I don't know if that was just hard feelings on my dad's part, or partly the truth. However, when Aunty Joyce and Uncle Ted put on their gladrags of a Saturday night, it was to travel in their little Ford Anglia to Binbrook to the Officer's Mess, no less. My mum and dad would be equally well attired, but for some reason, only be allowed into the Sergeant's Mess. My dad never got over the humiliation! One weekend, Uncle Ted issued an invitation to my mum and dad, to accompany him and Aunty Joyce to the Officer's Mess. My dad was apparently beside himself, and got very drunk and punched someone he thought was a bloody snob... so that was the end of that! My dad suffered from the most acute case of inverted snobbery but would rather die than admit it.

The point of telling you this is that when our parents went out at weekends, Sandra and I got to sleep over at each other's houses on a Saturday night. I loved being at her house best of all, because it always smelled of home-brew, home-baking and Axminster carpet. To this day, I remember the expensive smell of good carpet and will not rest until I've had at least one room floored with the stuff! I wanted our house to smell like Sandra's. Their kitchen was also bigger and was covered in Dandycord, a type of plastic rug that was supposed to be easy to clean. It was horrible stuff because if you dropped a piece of cheese, the cheese would become welded to the plastic and wouldn't budge, not even if you put a grenade under it!

Uncle Ted loved his home brew and was always banging on about what he would make it from next. Aunty Joyce said he would make wine out of toenail clippings if you let him! Thankfully, nobody ever did. Let him, that is. Some of it was good stuff but most of it would strip paint, and was lethal. Especially when given to my dad (who could drink the pub dry and then *drive* to the 'offy', or off-licence, for more).

Another of the joys of sleeping at Sandra's was that her bed was much more comfortable than mine. She had her own room, the house was warmer due to the central heating and my brother and sister weren't there. If we stayed at mine, we had to babysit as well as share my bedroom with my baby sister, and the next morning, my mother and father were usually in a drink-induced coma, and Sandra and I had to see to the kids.

Aunty Joyce was aware that all was not well in my life. She knew that my mother and father had a volatile relationship and she knew that my childhood was difficult and many times frightening. In her own way, I know she did love me, even though she found it difficult to show her emotions, and she made sure that when I was at their home, I was treated to a bit of kid comfort. She would tuck us up in bed and then she would make us a lovely breakfast the next day. Without exception, at around 10 o'clock on a Sunday morning, the phone would ring and it would be my mother demanding my return home to babysit again as she had to go out or to mind the kids while she did the neighbour's hair. Aunty Joyce would tell a little white lie, winking at us while she spoke to my mother saying, "They're not up yet, but as soon as they are I'll send her home." She would wink at me and offer another cup of tea and more toast, and I felt grateful for the time she bought me.

Sandra and I approached our teens with alacrity. It is amazing how resilient we can be as children. Despite the horrors of our different upbringings, as well as the good bits, we emerged into our teens with an optimistic outlook for the future.

I can't forget the day we discovered music. Aunty Joyce had an old Dansette record player in her dining room – oh, yes! Something else we didn't have. A record player. Or a dining room.

Aunty Joyce had delusions of grandeur and loved any excuse to get her dinner service out of mothballs, and dress the table with her posh cutlery! Sandy and I would be giggling our heads off when Aunty Joyce attempted to speak with a posh voice when they first got a phone. She would answer in her best telephone voice, adding 'H's' all over the place.

Ring, ring… "Ell-eow, this h'is Peppers 'ill three-four-Hoh," – you get the picture.

The first pop records we had were those big, black vinyl LPs (Long Players for those too young to remember vinyl records). Sand's sister had a couple of 45s (small versions of LPs) one of which was the Honeycombs, singing *Have I the Right* and the other was Pat Boone wailing *Speedy Gonzalez*. Sandra and I would thrash these two records to death until Aunty Joyce would beg for mercy and ban us from using the dining room. While we had the upper hand, though, we would make up elaborate dances and pretend we were going to be on Top of the Pops with Pan's People. Fat chance of that with Sandra's limited wardrobe! I sometimes snuck into my mother's extensive wardrobe and 'borrowed' a chain belt or a mini skirt and some high-heeled shoes for effect. Once, I even got away with her new leather coat and Sandra and I took turns being Emma Peel from the Avengers. Well, that was until she dug me in the ribs with her mum's brolly and I lamped her one with a platform boot.

One Saturday night, we 'borrowed' some new eyeliner after her sister had gone out with her boyfriend, and nearly blinded ourselves because we didn't have a clue how to use it. Sandra decided she would be the make-up artist and I was, as ever, the willing guinea pig. I had visions of emerging looking like Brigitte Bardot; all sultry, like a smouldering sex kitten. Instead, Sandra poked me in the eye with the brush, which was loaded with black, stinging gunk. My eyes watered so much I looked as if I'd been in a punch-up with Mick McManus (my granny's favourite wrestler).

## *The Youth Club – treat yerself, 'ave a coke!*

We really came of age when the Youth Club opened in the village. The Village was the posh shopping precinct, precursor to shopping malls but on a much smaller scale. Scartho, where we lived, housed many very nice people. They all did their shopping at The Village. There was Tates supermarket, a sort of latter day Waitrose but much more expensive. Then there was Verity's, the Chemist. They sold everything... even medicine! Then there was a hairdresser next to the Chinese takeaway and a very snooty dress shop called Verona's. Aunty Joyce would go in there and try on evening gowns prior to the Christmas do at the Officer's Mess. It was her once yearly treat to have a new frock and Uncle Ted smarted for weeks over the expense. He was very proud of his lovely wife, however, when she emerged on the night looking like a movie star. Anyway, we had to walk to The Village and it took 20 minutes at a brisk pace (especially if you had spotted Colin, who Sandra fancied like mad, on his yellow Lambretta, heading in the same direction). It took 30 minutes if you dawdled. It took hours if you had a pram full of kids and the week's shopping. I kid you not!

Anyway, my mum found out about the Youth Club. She fancied the bloke who ran it. She sweet-talked him into letting us join a few months earlier than the rules said we could. You were supposed to be thirteen and we were still twelve, but my mum spun him a brilliant sob story about how we were the only kids left to play on the streets and there were no other facilities, etc... he fell for it. Or he just fell for my mum's false eyelashes and black patent thigh boots? Anyway, we were in. Persuading Aunty Joyce to let Sandra go with me was another battle, but with perseverance, as they say, 'The Snail Reached the Ark'... and so we walked the quarter of a mile to our first ever outing to the Youth Club.

It was like being let loose in a sweet shop. There were records playing that were IN THE CHARTS! There was a tuck shop where you could get Coca Cola in a bottle, or orange squash, and Mars Bars and crisps. Occasionally, some bright spark would sneak in a can of shandy and be threatened with expulsion, but that was rare. When skinheads were all the rage, some of the more thuggish ones would be spotted around the corner, sharing a roll-up and would later swagger into the Youth Club as if they were James Dean. All in all, though, the youth leaders were a great bunch that seemed to understand spotty teenagers. We thought we were the bees knees.

Sandra, by now insisting I call her 'Sandy' on account of it being a much cooler name, and I were really good at dancing together. All those months in the dining room had taken care of that. We had perfected our own version of the Jive and we were very good at it. One night, the Youth Club announced its first disco and they were going to stage a dancing competition. Sandy and I hounded the lives out of our mothers for a new outfit each, and weren't surprised when we both turned up in the same dress. Actually, they weren't dresses at all, but nighties. They were gypsy-style that was fashionable that month, and mine was red and white and Sandy's was orange and white. Our mums had found them on the Freeman Street market for ten bob apiece. Oh well. Beggars can't be choosers… We were just happy to be getting out into the wide world and for a whole week, every night in the dining room, we put the Dansette through its paces, perfecting our moves. Friday night dawned and we even dared to ask if we could wear some make-up. My mum bought me a little tube of Miner's Blue Pearl eyeshadow and a black mascara *scream*, but she knew Aunty Joyce would never concede to letting Sandy wear 'that muck', so we got ready at my house and my mum helped us to get dolled up. We had to be pretty nifty to get back to my house before half past ten, so Sandy could have a wash and get rid of the evidence!

We floated on air to the Youth Club. The disco began, and after a few shuffles to *Chirpy Chirpy Cheep Cheep*, the dancing competition was announced. All those taking part had to line up on the dance floor. I say 'dance floor'; it was actually the five-a-side footie-cum-netball court, but with a few fairy lights and a mirror ball. We didn't complain.

Sandy and I began to Jive. Lucky for us the song they put on the turntable was *Yellow River* by Christie, so it was a suitable tempo – albeit a little slower than we had practiced – for the dance moves. We threw ourselves into the dancing, heart and soul, and as the record came to an end, she slid me through her legs and grabbed my hands and threw me over her shoulder to a momentous and thunderous applause. We had won! Our prize? A box of Meltis Newberry Fruits and a free coke each. Fred and Ginger, eat your heart out!

# *The Caravan*

Aunty Joyce and Uncle Ted had a caravan… yep, something else we didn't have. It was a static caravan and was sited on The Fitties Caravan Park in Humberston. Nobody knows how this place got its quirky name, and I guess nobody cared. Every summer Uncle Ted and Aunty Joyce would load up the 'van and I would get a couple of weeks holiday break. I lived for this break all year, and when the school holidays began, I was like a cat on a hot tin roof, breathless with excitement and checking the calendar every half hour. Sandy and I had our way of dealing with the excitement and every night leading up to 'the caravan' (shorthand for the experience), after school and after tea, we would curl up in her dad's Ford Anglia on her driveway, with the travel rug and a bag of jelly babies, and we would plan and talk and chat away about what we would do. 'The caravan' was planned with military precision, not just by Aunty Joyce and Uncle Ted, but by Sandy and me.

One of the joys of the holiday was the skating rink. It was nothing grand, it was just a covered concrete warehouse without walls, really, but that's where all the lads hung out. Also, her sister and her friends would come down there and they were all older and more sophisticated than we were. Sandy fancied a bloke called Bill Allenby and I fancied his mate, Vic (name eludes me). I was really shocked and embarrassed when a couple of years later, in secondary school, we were introduced to our new biology teacher. It was Vic wotsisname. Aaagghh!

One night, the grown-ups had gone off to the campsite funhouse known as the Foreshore Inn (whoever dreamed that one up deserves an Oscar, I don't think!). They had left Sandy and me in the caravan tucked up in our little beds with the gaslights dimmed, so that we could play cards or read. The transistor radio was coughing up any remote station it could lay a signal on, and we were happily shuffling a pack of cards when suddenly, the biggest bang shook the caravan. I've never seen anyone move as quickly as Sandy launched herself from her side of the 'van to mine. We huddled under the covers of my little bed for what seemed like hours until Aunty Joyce and Uncle Ted returned, a little merry. We were falling over each other dramatising the incident but soon returned to Earth with a bang when Uncle Ted chuckled, winked at Aunt Joyce and hiccupped, "Aww, it's probably just a rabbit!" We were hoping for something more sinister.

Sandy and I spent a lot of time scaring the wits out of one another, with our Tales of the Unexpected and in particular, our mutual fascination with UFOs or spaceships as they were known then. One cold Saturday night in November, we had been doing our usual babysitting stint for my mother, but I was sleeping over at Sandy's house for the night, so we had to walk round to her house in the dark. We had been talking about UFOs all night and pondering the mysteries of the Universe, which gave us the shivers up the spine and lighted the spark of curiosity within our hearts. Both of us were sure that other beings existed, but were not sure in which form. As we linked arms on the 10 minute walk back to her house, we suddenly became aware of a very strange light in the sky directly above us. It was like a bright silver ribbon that wove in and out of the sky...but the sky was cloudless although full of stars. We gawped at each other, and ran like crazy back to her house. Breathless and panting, we told Aunt J what we'd just seen. We didn't sleep much that night for excitement. Uncle Ted's usual response: "Yer must 'ave bin on the Portello again!"

## *The Barbara Mullen Appeal*

By Christmas 1969, Sandy and I were 13 years old. That year, there was a TV appeal launched by Save the Children. The presenter was a sweet little old Scottish lady called Barbara Mullen. She played a popular character in a sit-com called *Dr Finlay's Casebook* that my mum and gran watched religiously. Barbara Mullen was highlighting the plight of the poor, unfortunate children and beseeching the public to help by donating whatever they could, whenever they could.

The programme finished and our phone rang. It was Sandy. "Hey up, our Jewel. Did you see that Barbara Mullen thing on the telly, then?"

"Yes, I did," I sniffed, emotionally it had affected me. My siblings and I were always so lucky to find sacks full of presents on Christmas morning, and now we were tripping on guilt over the unfortunates that didn't even have parents. Sandy, it appears, had also been affected by the appeal.

We discussed what we could do to help and then we came up with an idea. "I know, let's go carol singing, and the money we get we'll send to the Barbara Mullen Appeal," suggested Sandy. I agreed wholeheartedly. It so happened that we'd had a massive fall of snow a few days earlier and in the deep and crisp and even of that snowy night, we sallied forth to do our bit. It was freezing cold but it was very pretty, as giant snowflakes floated softly to the ground and everywhere sparkled like icing sugar on a cake. We were both muffled up to the hilt, with gloves, hats and scarves and our feet were stuffed into our wellies with the aid of a couple of plastic bags, so our socks didn't get wet.

We sang our little hearts out at about thirty houses, and everyone very generously put a few pennies into our tin. They all seemed glad to do so after we explained that we were collecting for a special appeal. After each house, we would skip round the corner and tip out the money for a 'count up', and we soon had quite a bit in our fund. There was, however, one house left to go. It was the jewel in the crown, for it belonged to Miss Wold. Miss Wold was a spinster who lived in the biggest bungalow in the world. It was detached and it was rumoured that she was rich. She had a loathsome dog that barked incessantly if anyone went within two hundred yards of the house, so all the kids in the neighbourhood used to take great delight in finding new and innovative ways of making the dog go crazy. This silent night, this holy night, however, it was just the two of us. We took a deep breath and tiptoed as silently as we and the crunchy snow on the long driveway would allow. We were hoping to goodness not to make the stupid mutt bark, but at the opening chorus of *Away in a Manger*, as if on cue, the hound began to howl. We were caught between a rock and a hard place and mainly both wanted to leg it down the path, but suddenly the outside light snapped on, so we were caught like rabbits in the glare. The formidable shape of Miss Wold loomed into view behind the glass porch door. The door opened and in our minds, Sandy and

I could hear *Phantom of the Opera* playing as the door slowly creaked open (it didn't actually creak) and the creature inside revealed itself.

But it was only Miss Wold. She was about a hundred and fifty (possibly in reality she was only in her fifties). Her steely grey hair was permed into tight little curls that clung viciously to her head, and her face was pinched and lined as if she had been sucking lemons all day. She was only about five feet tall, but her aura of authority was gigantic and very scary. The song began to waver and die out, but Miss Wold barked at us, "Carry on, I'm listening!" – and so we found our second wind and carried on singing with gusto. As we finished singing, 'to live with thee there'... Miss Wold pierced us with her cold blue gaze and said, "If you think you're getting any money you can think again. It's not Christmas 'til 25$^{th}$ December. Come back then!" Then she promptly slammed the door in our faces and we slithered back down the driveway, 'V-signing' her all the way. We were determined to harass the life out of the dog after that.

Needless to say, we didn't go back. Neither did Barbara Mullen get our takings, all two pounds, three shillings and sixpence halfpenny. This was two years before decimalisation 'decimated' the good old pounds, shillings and pence. It was a fortune to us! However, we couldn't find a way of sending our money to her. Neither of us had a bank account and all other means of money transferring were for the over-18's. So we divided the spoils and spent the money on Christmas presents for our families instead. Oh well... the road to hell is paved with good intentions, or so they say!

*I know *Phantom of the Opera* hadn't been written then, but you get the meaning!

## Hey, Hey We're The Monkees...

There are many, many anecdotes I would love to recall from Sandy's and my shared history, but if I wrote them all down, you would be reading from now until Doomsday! I hope that by telling the stories that spring to mind most easily, you will get a sense of the depth of our friendship and how much we shared on every level and why ours was the most important friendship I had ever known.

The title of this book came to me because the things that bonded Sandy to me in life were the things that reconnected us after her passing. For instance, we both adored The Eagles in the 70's. They epitomised our dream of America with twingly, twangly country guitar riffs, and Take It Easy soft rock music, evoking pictures of deserts, canyons, sunshine and freedom. The Monkees were funny, zany guys, appealing to the funny and zany side of us. All members of the band were adored in equal measure, all being incredibly gorgeous and very fanciable. I recall being obsessed with Davy Jones, whilst Sandy was sure she was destined to marry Peter Tork! We both adored Micky Dolenz who sang most of the lead songs on their albums not only because he had a brilliant voice, but also because he was such a clown! His voice was (in our humble opinion) by far the best in the band. Mike Nesmith (Woolhat) was the gentle, quiet one with the funny woolly hat and was like your favourite big brother! Shame they never got to meet us, really…
*(well, not until much later… and then only one of us!)*

The desert has substantial significance because when we travelled to the U.S. in 1996, we had a momentous fight in the Mojave Desert, one that cathartically deepened our friendship and love and respect for one another. Things we had never said before were pulled out of the laundry bag, washed and aired, and although each of us was shocked and upset with what was said, once the clouds had cleared, the love between us was dusted down, polished up and set in stone. I now see that a true friendship needs to have these testing times in order to survive. Friendships that are based upon mutual ego-stroking are not friendships. Only when your friendship has been tempered in the fires of hell will you know you have something lasting and someone who truly loves you.

The desert was a fitting analogy for my grief after Sandy passed away. I felt I was in a dry, featureless world without an end in sight. Canyons featured in my emotional being as the sense of loss was so deep it seemed bottomless like a canyon. I was listening to a song on the radio one grey, wet and cold day. It was a country music tune, *Grand Canyon*, by Kathy Mattea. The lyrics were so poignant I was soon curled up in the foetal position, clutching my stomach and sobbing. The Grand Canyon was where my heart used to be. I didn't know how I would ever get over living without my lifelong friend and soul mate by my side.

After Sandy passed in '97, I frequently found myself in the emotional depths of the Grand Canyon, wandering through the searing, relentless desert that had parched my heart and although I wanted to soar like an Eagle again, my Monkee mind would not cease chattering about the past...

Anyhow... where were we? Oh, yes! I remember... we are not done with the Monkees yet! And so Saturday night was MONKEES NIGHT! Sandy and I had our routine mapped out, unless my mother ruined it! We would meet up at the corner of Southfield Avenue where she lived. It was round the corner from our house, but a good rendezvous point because the bus stop was at the top of this road. From there we would take the No. 9 bus into town and shop 'til we dropped. Shopping usually began in the music shop, back in the days when you could listen to your selected record in a little private booth, through huge Bakelite earphones. The pleasure we derived from such primitive technology remains unsurpassed even with today's improvements. Nowadays, I can listen to about 3,000 songs on a piece of machinery the size of a stamp! Incredible.

In the late 60's and early 70's The Monkees shot to fame, mainly through their television show, which was aired on a Saturday night in our neck of the woods. Sandy and I would listen to them most of the day in town, and then after buying a new eye shadow or a poster or some other 'clarts' (Aunt Joyce's word for everything for which she couldn't see the point) we would get back on the No. 9 bus to go home to her house for tea, and to watch 'the boys' on telly. Occasionally, and because we could never afford a whole album, we would borrow an album from a more affluent friend, but in those days there weren't many recording facilities to make copies of our favourite songs. These days, copying is much simpler and more widely available. So, because we had no access to recording facilities, we had to make do with listening to the songs as many times as we could and memorise the words. This drove Aunty Joyce to distraction, hearing the same 'racket' over and over again. Frequently, she would shout from the living room to the dining room, "Will you turn that racket down, I'm getting one of my headaches again," and we would have to exert some discipline over the volume control! Sandy had a particular talent for learning the words of songs very quickly, but I was a lot slower and couldn't always make out what the words were. It annoyed the hell out of her when I got the words wrong, but even after I had learned the 'right' ones I would continue to sing the wrong ones, just to wind her up. The usual result was a 'shoving and pushing' fight – semi-serious – culminating in us laughing ourselves silly on the dining room carpet.

Aunty Joyce, who was, despite her stern exterior, quite hopeless with confrontation, but she would intermittently pop her head in the room whereupon she would adopt her telephone voice (accompanied by the dreaded eyebrow), "Naow, naow, you two," (encompassing both of us). "Calm down or YOU will have to go home," (looking pointedly at me). We would bow our heads in deference until the door closed behind her, and then we would fall about giggling again. Rarely did I have to go home. Aunty Joyce was, underneath it all, a soft touch.

There were many favourite songs that Sandy and I jointly loved, but *Daydream Believer* was an all time favourite, as well as *Some Time in the Morning* and of course, *Look Out, Here Comes Tomorrow*, to which we used to mime the words and pretend we were on the Monkees TV show. *Look Out, Here Comes Tomorrow* has lyrics that refer to a couple of girls (Sandra and Mary), so Sandy felt obliged to claim the song for herself. I would mime the words until it came to the bit where Davy Jones sings breathlessly, 'Sandra... I love you' and I would mime, 'Sandra, I hate you' – and I'd get a swift dig in the ribs and the instant withdrawal of volume control privileges. Of course, this particular musical fantasy always ended with all of the Monkees falling hopelessly in love with us and whisking us away to live in America in fancy houses with swimming pools.

The Monkees were the primary object of our teenage affections for many years and today remain one of our all-time favourite bands. I have to say 'our' because every time Sandy wants to get my attention, I hear a Monkees song somewhere. I could be in the middle of the countryside and someone would come walking by with a radio playing. I swear it's true – this has happened to me. Much later, we discovered the Eagles and a marginally more mature obsession began. Interestingly, all our obsessions included America, the country. At the same time as The Eagles were being fêted, another band called America 'rode through the desert on a' *Horse With No Name*. We were smitten.

## Soaring with The Eagles

Their music took us to new heights of teenage awareness. We wanted to grow up, go to America and become hip, cool and trendy. We would visualise ourselves hanging out at an Eagles' concert, where we would be spotted in the crowd and invited to the after show party at some dusty dude ranch-cum-love-nest in the Wilds of the West. We were never too sure what happened after that; the anticipation of the dream being the best part. The dream always ended up with us both getting snogged senseless by our favourite band member – mine being Randy Meisner and Sandy's was Glen Frey - and being whisked away to a film star wedding, thereafter we would live Happily Ever After in a haze of bluesy-country guitar riffs and rib-eye steaks. Of course we would be on ranches, and they would be next door to one another. And yes, the customary film star home with swimming pool always featured at the end.

Oh, for a return to *The Innocence* which interestingly became a hit for Don Henley (of the Eagles).

In 1972, *Take It Easy* was released and it became our signature tune. Little did I realise how significant this beautiful song would become a few years later.

## The Trouble with Tribbles – the Stuff of Star Trek!

Of course, it has to be said that as teenage girls, obsessions were part of growing up. One of our obsessions was Star Trek. One episode stands out above the others for comic value, although Sandy and I thought that Gene Roddenberry was an unsung visionary. In my line of work I recognise pure genius when I feel it, and Gene Roddenberry – creator of Star Trek – was a genius.

The Trouble with Tribbles was simply one of the funniest episodes ever produced by the Star Trek team. The story centred around these little furry things that were very cute and made a sort of *tribbling*e sound, not unlike the old Trimphone of the 70's. My mother had to have one of those and they were at best a fashion statement for the modern housewife, and at worst a design nightmare with a pathetic ring tone any budgie could imitate. Well, ours did, to his amusement and my mother's rage.

However, let us return to the Enterprise. Sandy loved Captain James T Kirk aka William Shatner. I was more enamoured by Spock. Go figure! We never missed an episode and years later when the new generation series was aired, Sandy remained resolutely loyal to the original crew.

We howled with laughter over the antics of the Tribbles and the crew of the Enterprise, and made ourselves sick laughing as we re-enacted the scene in Aunt Joyce's dining room. Sandy had been a bridesmaid at her sister's wedding in 1976. I was supposed to be the other bridesmaid, but was heavily pregnant with my first child and so had to bow out of the wedding duties. Sandy was outraged at Jan for making her wear a pair of swansdown ear muffs on a fluffy headband and I was grateful for small mercies. I didn't have to wear them as well. She said the headgear made her look like a bloody cabbage patch doll.

Those wonderful ear muffs came in pretty handy, however, when transmuted into Tribbles. Sandy dismantled the headband, divested it of its fluffy endpieces and voila! The scene was complete. We would chase one another round the dining room squeaking like a couple of idiots until we dropped, exhausted from laughing. Uncle Ted said we were 'a couple of bloody lunatics'. Nuff said!

## *The Dining Room*

I can still, to this day, smell my Aunty Joyce's dining room. It was a mixture of home-brew, fresh fruit and Axminster carpet with a bit of furniture polish for good measure! What a heady combination! I think Aunty Joyce just wanted to have a 'posh dining room' as they had never had one when they lived in Wellington Street. The best they had was the front parlour, which nobody was allowed to access, unless they had died! This room was kept for 'best' by most housewives in 'two-up, two-down' accommodation, pre and post war. It was where they laid out their deceased, as far as I can remember. It was hallowed ground and woe betide you if ever you set foot in the 'best room'. However, in the new house in Southfield Avenue, they had four bedrooms and two reception rooms. I think Aunty Joyce felt she had been elevated to royal status having this much room. It gave her a false sense of nobility! However, as I said before, she was a softie at heart and she never minded Sandy and me turning her best room into a discotheque on a Saturday or Sunday afternoon, as long as we kept it reasonably tidy and didn't damage anything. She was very proud of her dining table, which she polished to a high glossy shine, and she loved her knick-knack shelf, with all the little china figurines and cut glass rosebud vases. Having a bit of cut glass gave her a sense of aristocracy, for some reason. She felt she was a 'cut above', so to speak. Aww... bless her.

I think this is why I have tried to re-create in my own home the wonderful, warm sense of nostalgia and well-being that was given to me by Aunty Joyce and her dining room. I have furnished my own 1930's dining room with an old utility-style, drop-leaf dining table and chairs, and a china cabinet filled to bursting with cut glass and china and little knick-knacks. I make sure there is always a bowl of fruit in there, as well, so that I can nip in and out and inhale my Aunty Joyce once more. I only wish I had been able to tell her how much she meant to me, while she was alive, but I'm sure she knows now.

One Sunday afternoon, after a vigorous practice session, and drunk with our own creativity, we were attempting to incorporate some very innovative and risqué moves into our Jive routine. Sandy got a little bit over-enthusiastic and in an attempt to throw me over her shoulder, slide me down her back and through her legs, forgot the friction element of the Axminster carpet and her socks. As her socks slid down her feet, she twisted round on the overhang, tripped and fell headlong into Aunty Joyce's brand new Gas Miser... we heard a sound that brought us swiftly to our senses and when we realised we'd actually cracked one of the important bits, we sobered up instantly! "Oh, my bloody God," whispered Sandy, "she will kill us."

"Don't bother calling on God," says I. "He won't bloody well help us now. I'm off home before she finds out!" and with that,

I hastily pulled on my shoes and shot off down the drive. Aunty Joyce looked puzzled as she peered out of the sitting room window at my departing figure, but assumed we'd had an argument, which wasn't uncommon. When I got home, I felt a bit guilty about leaving Sand to take the rap, so I rang her and asked if our little misdemeanour had been discovered yet.

"No, but it's only a matter of time," she replied. We decided that discretion was the better part of valour and agreed to play dumb if questioned.

I don't know if anyone remembers Gas Misers, but they had these little radiant panels that lit up when the gas flame was ignited. They resembled small chalk ladders. They were the important bit of the fire, because they were the bits that heated up and kept you warm. They were notoriously fragile and you only had to sneeze on them for them to show a hairline crack in no time.

About a week passed, with Sandy and I on tenterhooks, waiting for the moment our dastardly deed was discovered, but on the following Saturday, Aunty Joyce asked if we would like to play in the dining room again, while she popped to the shops. Warily, Sandy and I shuffled into the dining room and Aunty Joyce, having one of her 'nicer days' (no headache in evidence) kindly offered to plug in the Dansette for us before she went out. As she opened the lid of the record player, which was by the side of the fireplace, the plug, which had been sitting on the top of the lid, shot off at an angle, and crashed into the front of the Gas Miser!!!

There was a moment when nobody breathed... then Aunty Joyce, with a look of sheer horror on her face, turned to us and said, "I've broken the bloody radiant panel. Look, there's the crack... Oh, my God... DO. NOT. SAY. A. WORD. Either of you. Or I'll strangle you!" It would seem that Aunty Joyce's fear of what Uncle Ted would say and do was greater than our fear of her. It was a hollow victory...

# Part 2

## 'What the Caterpillar Perceives as the End, the Butterfly Perceives as the Beginning'

Nothing prepares you for the physical death of a loved one. Nothing.

One minute, a vibrant personality is alive and living out its life's experiences, and the next minute, it's gone.

The shock that hits you following the sudden death of somebody you love, feels like an electric cable carrying thousands of volts has struck you. At first, numbness surrounds your emotions like a safety blanket. Moving through life on auto-pilot, you find yourself attending to daily tasks, thinking only thoughts you absolutely need to think in order to deal with the practicalities.

You descend into denial. This is part of the shock, and it is usual to invalidate what has happened, with logic. 'So-and-so couldn't be dead, because I only saw her/him yesterday'.

Whether you last saw so-and-so two days, two weeks or two years ago is irrelevant. It is unbelievable, however, that in such a short space of time, somebody you knew has vacated that thing we know as 'a body' and gone, gone, gone…. Gone – where the hell have they gone?

In a while, reality sets in and you realise you can no longer ignore the fact that so-and-so is not coming back. You can never see, phone, talk to, or call round upon them ever again. You can never hear their voice, laugh with them, cry with them, or fall out with them. They are gone, for good.

One morning you wake up with that dreadful white-hot burning sensation in the pit of your stomach and the realisation that you are without this person in your life. They have died, and you are here, alone, without them. You don't have them, but you have a gaping, yawning chasm in your solar plexus as big as the Grand Canyon. Everything in life takes on a dull, grey tinge. The colour seems to have faded out of your world almost overnight. It feels like the washing machine has been set on too hot a wash, and all the things in the machine have come out in the same grey, blue, bland, nothing colour.

You hear a song on the radio, and you think: Oh! I'll just phone 'so-and-so', she/he likes this one… and then the bleak reality hits you in the face again.

It is winter all year round.

You don't know how you are going to carry on living a 'normal' life without so-and-so. You might not have even seen whoever it was for some time. You might not have seen them on a regular basis. You didn't need to. You always knew they were going to be there for you. This is especially true if your loved one was the same age as you.

You don't realise it, but slowly and painfully, you crawl into a cocoon of depression. It is a different experience for each individual, but for me, this cocoon crept slowly over me, over a period of two years.

My particular 'so-and-so' died unexpectedly. Ironically, a few weeks later, anguish and pain hit me again, as I watched the death of a TV soap star acted out in Coronation Street. The character died of a deep vein thrombosis, just like Sandy did. I howled like a wounded animal and sobbed uncontrollably, rocking like a child. There was nowhere to take this pain.

It is of no particular consequence whether or not you have a belief system or religion to cushion you. As I invariably found, my encounter with Sandy's death made me re-examine everything I had ever believed in. To begin with I threw out the baby with the bathwater, so to speak. I lived in my pyjamas and dressing gown, and didn't give two hoots about how I looked. On some days I didn't give a damn if I didn't actually get out of bed at all.

I was very fortunate to have found, at that time, a very understanding partner. He didn't try to shake me out of whatever I was experiencing. He wasn't fazed by my depression and he certainly wasn't afraid of it. He never once told me to 'pull myself together', 'get a grip', or anything similarly insensitive.

As anyone who has undergone depression knows, it is not simply a matter of 'pulling oneself together'.

My advice to anyone who knows someone in the process of grieving is to let them Be. Allow them to experience their sorrow, in the fullest sense they possibly can. For it is certainly true to say that the only way out is through. I know this works, because it is how I managed my situation.

I couldn't run away from my feelings if I'd tried. They were too deep, too painful and too acute.

Then one day the floodgates opened. I cried for what seemed like weeks and months, and I didn't think I was ever going to stop. These tears were such a relief. It felt like a dam had burst at long last, and I could begin to flow again with life in general, instead of being reined in behind a huge wall.

Three years later, I considered myself over the worst. It was only about eighteen months after Sandy's death that I decided to consult a bereavement counsellor, but this step was a wise move forward. Maybe I could have taken this line of action sooner, but I felt it came at the right time for me.

Nobody can say how long it will take another to heal from grief and loss. Each one is different. At the time of writing, I have now been without my Sandy, in the physical sense of the word, for 13 years. Only now do I consider myself 'over the worst', however I can still get a lump in my heart when I hear 'our song', or see someone who knew us both. That is good. One must retain good memories, not erase every trace of this valuable life form.

*"The only sure thing is that the sun is shining behind the clouds, and it will surely come out again, one day." (Julie, September 1999.)*

## Shot through the heart

It was a warm, summer day in June/July time and I'd just had a phone call that had shocked me to the core. My American boyfriend, whom I'd not heard from in some time, and to whom I had written, breaking off our fledgling relationship, had called me out of the blue asking me to go to America and live with him. I had not expected to hear from him again, and I had already met Paul who was to become my long-term partner. We were friends at this stage, but I was hoping things might develop into something more permanent.

I was certainly not prepared to receive this proposal from afar, and my head was spinning and my heart was in a whirl. I went to the beach for a long walk and to think about what to do, and I decided I needed to call Sandy and talk it over with her. She was my rock, and I knew she would listen to me and not judge or try to tell me what to do, but would provide a good sounding board from which I could bounce some thoughts and reach a conclusion.

I went to the nearest phone box and called her. All I said was, "I need my Sand."

And she said, "You need to come home to sort this out," then she downed tools, jumped into her car and travelled the few miles from her house to pick me up and take me 'home'. I spent a lot of time at Sandy's house when we were kids. It was my refuge and my sanctuary at times, and I used to want to live there because we could just be kids together. At my house, I always seemed to have to look after my little brother and sister, or do the housework for mum or help out in some other way, usually babysitting. Sandy usually did these things with me, but I know her mum disapproved of the way my mum ran our household!

Sandy and I discussed this strange and unexpected proposal at length, and at the end of the discussion she said to me, "Well luvvie, if you decide to go, it will give me an excuse to get on a plane and come visit America again."

I wanted to cry, because that was just typical of her; always thinking of someone else not herself. I hugged her and said, "But I don't want to leave you, and I also want you to know that wherever I am in the world, if you need me, I'll be right here," and I touched my heart and hers in the way that Elliott and ET exchanged their love in the movie, ET (a favourite of Sandy's and mine).

We then decided to fire up the barbecue, usually reserved for Bonfire Night when we'd eat like pigs and then send up three rockets, one for her, one for me and one for 'absent friends'. We were both hungry and whilst we prepared the food and set the charcoal to burn, I noticed that she didn't seem quite right. She had to sit down more than once, as she was out of breath, and when I questioned her she fobbed me off with something about having a 'panic attack'.

I was very concerned, as this apparently kept happening and it was bothering her. She hadn't said anything to me, as I know that she knew I would go on at her to go see her GP. She hated 'medical shenanigans', having spent most of her life in and out of hospitals having surgical repair work done to her face.

"Sand, this is no effing panic attack," I said, "tell me how you have been feeling."

She described a shortness of breath and dizziness and aches and pains in her legs and said it had been particularly bad in the past week.

I was very disturbed, and after we'd eaten, we decided to take a short walk to the local garage, as was part of our getting together ritual, to get goodies and crisps for the evening so we could chill out, watch TV and relax. We hadn't walked more than a few yards up the road when Sandy had to stop and sit on a wall to draw breath. She insisted that she was okay and wanted to continue walking, so we did, but the 20-minute walk there and back took over an hour.

Later that evening, we sat down to watch a movie of our favourite programme, *Star Trek*, when she cried out and clutched at her side. She was in a lot of pain, and said she felt like she had a severe stitch in her side and again, she had difficulty getting her breath. I was quite alarmed by now and I didn't know what to do, so I tried to make her as comfortable as I could and I massaged her back and side for her until she felt the pain subside. Not long after, we decided to go to bed.

The next morning, after a restless night, we got up for breakfast and she didn't look too bright. Something wasn't right, but I couldn't put my finger on what it was. She and I looked out at her beloved garden and mused upon how abundant it was this year. She told me her tomatoes had overtaken her neighbour's in size, colour and quantity this year, and remarked how incredibly big the vegetables had grown, too. I had to agree, they looked amazing. She picked up the garden knife and said, "Wait there, I'll go cut you some veg... don't worry about the winter, because I'll freeze some and we'll have enough to keep us both going!" It touched me deeply that she had thought about me in this way, as at that time, I was not working and was finding it difficult to make ends meet.

As I watched her shuffle down the garden path, the path that I'd watched her lovely dad, my Uncle Ted, shuffle down some many times, I felt something wash over me that didn't feel good at all. An

49

unbearable sadness weighed upon my heart, and a chill ran down my spine. I didn't know why but I wanted to cry. As she struggled up the winding little path she was carrying one of the hugest cauliflowers I'd ever seen. It must have been three feet across and no kidding! What I noticed more than the gigantic vegetable was that my lovely girl seemed so frail... for a split second I felt like I was seeing a ghost.

She carried the cauli into the kitchen and fussed around trying to find a bag. A chill went through me again.

"Sandy, please put that down and come here," I said, my voice breaking.

She looked at me and I swear our souls smiled at one another for a millisecond, and I looked into those sparkling blue eyes and reflected back at me was 'tired and weary and resigned'. I wrapped her in my arms and tried not to cry.

"Sand... don't leave me. You promise me you won't go anywhere, will you?" which was an odd thing to say to someone. Sandy was the stable one and I was always flitting off somewhere. For goodness sake, this was the purpose of my weekend visit!

"Don't be daft," she said, "I'm not going anywhere." Momentarily, her voice seemed to be coming from a different dimension, from a place where I felt I couldn't reach her. Simultaneously, I was scared, but the feeling passed and I pulled myself back to the present.

I made her promise me she would go to the doctor the following week and I said that if she hadn't made an appointment by Tuesday, I would drag her there myself. She promised that she would and we hugged and I told her that I loved her very much and that I didn't think I could bear it if anything happened to her.

She sorted out the vegetables, and bundled me into her car ready to drive me home. As she dropped me at the door of my flat, I kissed her goodbye and said, "Now don't you forget, RING THE DOCTOR ON MONDAY!!!" and she said she would.

The bitter irony of words, and situations and scenarios when played back on the movie screen of our minds crushes my heart to this day. How could I possibly have known that this was the last weekend I would ever spend with my girl?

On the following Monday, I was busy tidying up the flat and doing other things and the day flew by before I realised that I hadn't called Sandy. I reminded myself that tomorrow I would call her and see if she'd kept her promise. The next day, I tried to call but got no answer, which wasn't unusual as she spent a lot of time in the garden and sometimes ignored the phone! I knew she would call me later if I left a message.

I hadn't seen anyone that day, because my mum and dad had gone to Jersey for their two-week holiday and my other friends were either busy or working. Paul, whom I had only recently met and become friends with, was working his night shift so I decided to have an early night.

At 10:30 that night, there was a persistent knocking on the front door. I didn't know who it was, and I tried to look out of the window to see who could be calling so late. The knocking persisted and as there was nobody else in the other flats of the complex in which I lived, I decided to go downstairs and see who it was.

A policeman and woman were standing on the step, and as I opened the door, they asked if I knew of the whereabouts of 'Julie Lauder'…

"That's me," I replied, somewhat puzzled. "How may I help you?"

"Do you know someone called Sandra Coulbeck?" the woman PC asked me.

"Yes I do, she's my cousin – why, what's she done?" I asked semi-jokingly.

"Could we step inside, please, ma'am. I'm afraid we have some rather bad news for you," said the PC… after which things became rather blurry and distant and I heard, from a distance, someone saying, "I'm afraid Miss Coulbeck has died…"

*(I'm falling… falling…falling from a great height, into an abyss of great black depth and I don't care. Unfamiliar voices are ringing in my ears and I can't really hear them, but what they are saying is incomprehensible to me and I protest, weakly at first, then more strongly. I am offered cups of tea and I say "No thank you, I have to go out," and I don't know where I have to go to, I don't know what to do or where to run)…*

The two constables were very concerned and asked if I had anyone I could be with.

"Yes – Sandy, my Sandy... she's all I've got... but ..." and suddenly, nothing made sense anymore.

Only when they felt I'd be okay to be left alone did the kind people decide it was okay to leave, and I reassured them that I wouldn't harm myself or anyone else, but stressed that I did wish to be left alone. And left alone in the empty flat, bereft of all rhyme and reason and, clad only in my pyjamas and dressing gown, I suddenly had this urge to get dressed and run for as long as I could run without stopping...

I dragged on some jeans and a jumper and stuffed my feet into a pair of old trainers, then I walked outside into the dark, starry night. I was looking for some kind of normality. I needed a touchstone because life suddenly felt surreal. The only money I had in my jeans pocket was a fifty pence piece. I desperately needed to talk to someone. Anyone. I rang my sister who lived in Liverpool, and broke down, sobbing incoherently. My sister was miles away, so was Mum and for this awful time, I was alone on the planet.

I left the call box and ran and ran. Running felt better because while I was running, I couldn't notice what was going on inside of me. I ran all the way without stopping, or taking a breath, to Paul's house and stood there, knowing full well he wasn't in. I saw a light somewhere inside, and started banging and banging on the door, sobbing and sobbing and wishing and praying for him to somehow, miraculously appear and hold me and tell me it'd all been a bad dream.

I collapsed in the porch, feeling desolate, frightened and not knowing where to turn, but then I remembered someone I could possibly call on. My friend, David, lived in town and I figured he would be at home. This meant going back to the flat to get more money, as I didn't have a landline installed. I was terrified to go back indoors, because my life force had vacated the premises. I grabbed some money and ran back to the phone box again, and called David's house. Thank God he was in, and he and his mother, God bless them, came straight away and put me in the car and took me back to their house.

I spent the whole night in a world of nightmares and bad dreams, drifting in and out of consciousness, waking temporarily now and again to feel the crushing pain of loss in my solar plexus and the place where my heart used to be. I dreamed about Sandy, and I woke up to hug her and she wasn't there, and I didn't want anyone else to be there and I couldn't stop crying.

Never have I felt such devastating pain. Never.

I stayed at David's house for the next two or three days, because I couldn't go back to the flat. I was experiencing the worst nightmare of my life from which, unfortunately, I couldn't wake up.

All I knew was that Sandy had been in my life one weekend and two days later, she was out of it forever and I didn't want to wake up in a world without her in it.

The next few days passed in a haze as Sandy's older sister was contacted and funeral arrangements took place. I learned through others that it was to be a cremation. It wasn't what I wanted for Sandy, but as there was some bad feeling between her sister and me, which couldn't, at that time, be sorted out amicably, I felt I had no say in the matter. Shame on both of us…

One thing that touched my heart and soul forever was the gorgeous basket of flowers that arrived at my flat from two dear friends, Giovanna and Val, whom Sandy and I had met on our trip to America the previous year. I will never forget their empathy, kindness and compassion. Drying my tears for the umpteenth time, I went to fetch the giant sunflowers I had ordered at the local florist's. The lady in there was so warm and again, very empathetic, and when I told her I needed sunflowers, she set about sourcing them, on special order from Holland, and true to her word they arrived within the week. I placed my sunflower with Sandy's other flowers at the crematorium. She reminded me of a big, beautiful sunflower. Bright, beautiful and despite everything she'd gone through, always kept her beautiful face to the sunshine.

The funeral, in stark contrast to the bright shining light that was Sandy, was a cold and formal affair. I wanted a Memorial Service attended by all the people who loved her most, so that her presence could be validated by warm and wonderful memories of her brief life. She touched many people with her winsome ways and she didn't even know it. Sadly, there wasn't even a funeral reception afterwards. Mourners departed the crematorium and went home, which only added to my grief and feelings of invisibility. I never managed to speak to Sandy's sister again after that and I am so sorry that we haven't reconciled our misunderstandings… I hope she will read this someday, and know that my heart goes out to her and my best wishes are with her always.

A few of us did decide to go back to my flat and have our own memorial service, and I am eternally grateful that Pat and Jill and Drene and David spent that time with me, playing Sandy songs and music from 'our era', the 70's, and remembering the good times and generally getting rip-roaringly, mind-numbingly drunk! Sandy would have approved of this wake, loving her tipple as she did!

Days passed as days do and somehow I managed to carry on functioning. At this time, Paul became more of a friend to me and our relationship blossomed. I have always said that Sandy must have sent him to me because I do not know how I would have survived had it not been for his support and his love.

I reiterate, he never once told me to 'pull myself together' and he never once tried to stop my tears or make me go to the doctor for pills to 'numb the pain'. He embraced my bereavement and grieving process and stood by me with the heart of a lion, and I will always love him and respect him for what he gave me. He didn't even know Sandy, but he knew what she meant to me and he respected fully what her life and our relationship had been to me.

In time, it became clear that Paul was a budding and rather brilliant medium himself, through which Sandy chose to speak to me when I needed her the most. I have many stories and anecdotes, some of which I will share with you, of how Sandy communicated with me through Paul. I know she would have liked Paul because he's a lot like her dad, my Uncle Ted! Steadfast, reliable and trustworthy. Above all, he was there for me when I needed his constancy the most.

I feel it necessary to acquaint you with how Sandy and I continued our relationship 'beyond the grave' and how our communications gave birth to the writing of this book. I give you these words with all my love… from Sandy and me, to you.

## *Losing Uncle Ted*

After Uncle Ted died, sometime in the 1980's, Sandy was inconsolable. Her dad was her hero! To lose him was like losing a limb. Of course, she also loved her mum very dearly, and when Aunty Joyce passed away at a fairly young age, Sandy was Uncle Ted's 'little rock'. Sadly, there had been a bit of a family upset, resulting in a rift between Jan, Sandy and Uncle Ted. I don't really know what it was about, but I know it must have been very hard for all of them, in one way and another. For whatever reason, Sandy didn't feel she could turn to her sister for comfort and support, but that might have been more about Sandy's perspective on things, rather than Jan's unwillingness to meet halfway.

Sometimes, in the middle of the night, she would call me and just sob for hours, and all I could do was listen. Her plaintive cries of, "Where's Daddy gone?" ripped through me, as I didn't have the answers. She wanted to know why she couldn't see him or hug him anymore... My beliefs were not enough for her or for me and I wished I could tell her something that would make her feel better. I could only conclude that she was too shrouded in grief to hear or see anything through her veil of tears. God, how I wish I'd known how she felt so I could have supported her better, but I didn't. Not until she left me...

## *The Gift of Time*

When Sandy telephoned me to tell me the devastating news that Uncle Ted, my hero, was on his way out, I cried like a baby. I was living in Yorkshire at the time, but wanted to get in the car and go see them right away. However, Uncle Ted was a proud man, and Sandy was very protective of him. He didn't want anyone to see him in a state of illness, so she kindly asked me not to visit at that time, which I respected. I learned that Uncle Ted had lost a lot of weight rather rapidly, and was a shadow of his former self. Naturally, being a strapping big handsome chap, he did not want anyone to see his decline.

I didn't know what to do. I felt lost and for the first time I also felt the stirrings of what it was like to be losing someone close. As anyone who has been in this situation will know, it brings your own mortality into question rather uncomfortably.

Flashbacks to happy childhood scenes flickered through my mind like a movie, and memories filled with Uncle Ted and his Ford Anglia and Aunt Joyce's Sunday tea flooded through me. Aunt Joyce's home-made bread was the source of great amusement. One incident in particular stands out for me as it landed me in hospital. (Well, it turned out I had appendicitis, but we always said it was Aunt Joyce's bread that started it). One Sunday, Aunt J presented Sandy and I with a plate of her freshly baked bread buns filled with cold chicken.

That night, I woke up in agony, very sick indeed. I was terrified. My mum was so scared that she called 999 and about 15 minutes later I was diagnosed with acute appendicitis (there was nothing 'cute' about it, let me tell you!) Later, when Sandy came to visit me in the hospital, she literally had me in stitches making me laugh when she suggested that her dear mother's bread buns might have been the cause! Aunt Joyce, as usual, was *not amused*!

My attendance at school was something of a family joke, because I was never at school if I could help it. I had hated school from the first day I was taken there. I can remember my mum sneaking off and the teacher attempting to pacify me and then I tipped up the sand tray before tipping up the water tray and soaking several other infants. I screamed like a stuck pig until granny came to fetch me at dinner time. I thought that was it and when I had to go back again, I bit the teacher and kicked the headmistress. Hmm... I still get twitchy around authority figures!

When Sandy and I started secondary school, Uncle Ted took us in the Ford Popular (a bigger upgrade from the tiny Ford Anglia) – me to the bus stop, and Sandy to her school. The vinyl seats were lovely and cool in the summer but cold as hell in the winter. We went to different schools, which were about 3 miles apart. It was imperative that we got to my bus stop on time, because the bus left at 8:30am, and if I didn't catch it, I would be late for school. Occasionally, if Uncle Ted was in a bad mood, or if Sandy had dragged her heels over breakfast, I would be in bother. I hated it and to this day, I get the same old feeling in my gut if I'm late for anything, and have developed the knack of turning up for appointments at least a quarter of an hour early.

My school absences were always given spotlight treatment by Uncle Ted and I would dread going round to Sandy's house for a lift on the next school morning after an absence. I hated it but Uncle Ted's sarcasm – which he mistook for wit – was always directed at me. "You'll end up on that bloody fish finger line at Bird's Eye if you don't go to school," he would quip every time, wagging his engine oil-stained finger at me. He disapproved of my mother's lack of discipline but chose to channel his frustration through me. I always felt like a worm on the end of a hook and was glad when we got to the bus stop and I could escape.

Years later, I can still recall the day I landed a very prestigious job in Yorkshire. I phoned Sandy with the good news and said, "Be sure and tell your dad. And tell him it's MILES FROM THE BLOODY FISH FINGER LINE!' As it turned out, Uncle Ted was as proud of my achievement as if I was his own daughter. I often used to wish I was.

The time frame is a little hazy now, but between Uncle Ted's diagnosis of bowel cancer and his demise, time was swift and kind. If I remember rightly, it was on Sandy's birthday, before he died he bought Sandy a watch. He said, "I can't give you time babby (his pet name for her) but I can try and buy you some."

Time is the most precious gift you can give anyone, as Sandy later taught me.

A year after Uncle Ted's death, Sandy and I had one of our Saturday trips into town. It was a little ritual we had enjoyed since we were old enough to be let out alone. As teenagers, it was a great adventure to go into town on the bus to buy the latest chart hit, or some new makeup. Aunt Joyce's voice would ring in our ears on the way out of her house, "Don't speak to any strangers and come home for 5. I'll have your teas ready for you."

We would stay in town for ages, 'til it was time to catch the bus home, then we would get home to Sandy's in time for tea and to watch The Monkees on TV. The Monkees were our idols! We were obsessed with listening to everything they ever sang, as teenagers are. I was passionately in love with Davy Jones and Sandy was in love with Peter Tork. It was sacrilege not to be home in time to watch The Monkees!

At this particular time, I was lodging at my mum's house, having moved back home to Cleethorpes from Yorkshire, following a very painful divorce.

Sandy rang to say she would pick me up there. When she arrived, she asked me if I'd mind going with her to the travel agency in town where she intended booking a holiday. I was excited to be included because I felt she needed a break after all she'd been through. We headed for the travel shop. I sat in the chair beside Sandy as she and the agent checked out a number of options. She had decided to take a trip to America. Oh my God! America!! I was so excited for her... I couldn't believe she would take on such a trip alone, but she'd changed and grown a lot in the time since Uncle Ted had gone, and I guessed this was all part of the 'new Sandy'... It might as well have been my own trip I was planning, the thrill was just as big. She ummed and ahhed, and occasionally turned to me to ask a few questions. I tried to stay detached but interested as I wanted to help her get the best deal. She decided on something entitled the 'West Coast Aloha'. This was an assisted coach tour of 11 days and the last four days of the trip would be spent in Hawaii. I could barely contain myself... and I wished I was going. America had been our childhood fantasy, and she was finally making a dream come true.

Sandy chose the holiday and asked the agent to book two places for the trip commencing 1$^{st}$ August 1996. She paid the deposit and smiled at me.

"Wow, Sand... that is bloody brilliant. Wow. Well done you. By the way, who are you going with?" I asked.

"You," she grinned. "Well, that's if you want to come, of course!"

I was totally lost for words. I could not believe what she had just said. We danced around, and hugged and laughed and cried and danced around again, before I dragged her into the nearest bar for a medicinal brandy, or three! My heart was beating wildly and the enormity of her generosity hit me in the heart.

When it had sunk in, I started to cry. I said to her, "Sandy, I can never repay you for this. You have no idea what this means to me."

"You already paid me forward," she said gently. "After Dad died, you saved my life. You gave me the greatest gift of all… your time."

I had not known that when I called the broken little girl who was in pieces after Uncle Ted's funeral, to ask her to come to stay with me in Ilkley for a few days, what that gesture had meant to her. For the three days she was at my house, I cosseted her and pampered her and wrapped her in blankets. I was interested in reflexology at the time, and I treated her to a foot bath and massage. I could feel some kind of healing energy pouring into her from me, but to my mind it was simply the Love I felt for her. Love heals all wounds, nothing else. If all I could give her was my time and energy, then she was going to have an overdose of it.

I asked her again why she wanted to do this and she said, "Well, consider it Dad's gift to you because he isn't here to give it to you himself. I know it is what he would have wanted… the thing is, I feel I want to give you back a piece of your childhood." Nobody could ever know what that meant to me. Only Sandy.

1st August couldn't come quick enough for us and a week prior to our visit to the Big Country, we walked along Cleethorpes beach arm in arm, talking excitedly about our lifetime dream. We recalled happily, that when we were just two little girls, with our whole lives ahead of us, we planned to 'go to 'Merica when we were grown up'. We would sit and watch all the cowboy movies including an all time favourite, The Big Country. We made believe we were cowgirls, riding the range on the back of my granny's horsehair sofa and using our skipping ropes for reins!

I believe this was my proof that dreams really do come true…

The night of 31st July I drove over to Sandy's house to stay the night, as we were flying the next day. Neither of us could sleep. Like Morecambe and Wise, we slept like two big kids in her new king sized bed. There was very little sleep. Our flight from Terminal 1, Heathrow, departed at 10 o'clock, and a taxi had been booked to transport us. We were travelling in style! We got up at about three in the morning too excited to do little except feel nauseous and certainly not ready to eat anything. I found out much later that Sandy was absolutely terrified of flying, but she never mentioned a word to me.

The airport was bustling with travellers. Neither Sandy nor I had ever been to Heathrow, and the atmosphere was electric. Everyone was going somewhere exciting and there was a comfort in the organised chaos. We looked around every shop in the airport, and then did the Duty Free bit, and before we knew it, our flight was being called.

As we boarded the huge plane, we held hands like two little girls and screamed out, "YEE HAW!!!" and then we settled into our seats ready for take-off.

As the plane roared into action, I looked at Sandy and she was as white as a sheet. I took her hand, which was gripping the seat, and I said, "It's okay. I'm here and we'll be alright."

We *were* alright and we really enjoyed the flight, most of which she slept through and I talked through, to anyone I could talk to. I just couldn't contain my excitement. After twelve long hours we landed in San Francisco and Sandy's face, as we flew over Golden Gate Bridge, was indescribable. We just grinned at one another like two idiots and allowed our feet to Happy Dance underneath the plane seats.

## *Saddle up the stove, honey. We're gonna ride the range tonight!*

San Francisco was cold. When we landed we hadn't expected it to be chilly, and neither of us had brought a woolly, as we expected America to be hot! How naïve is that? She looked at me and grinned. "We could have bloody well stayed at home for this weather," she grumbled.

I laughed and said, "Never mind. Sand, WE ARE IN AMERICA! Let's enjoy every second."

We did enjoy every second, but neither of us had reckoned on jet lag. Or the effect tiredness has on your emotions. On the third day we were up at the crack of dawn to breakfast and meet up with the party of people that were to become our 'travel family' for the next fortnight. We all said hello to one another as we boarded the luxury coach for the next stop on the tour, Fresno. After an overnight stay in beautiful Fresno, we were headed to the awesome Yosemite National Park.

That was when the trip really began for us. The most striking thing to us was the big sky! We had never seen sky like it, it was endless and blue. Clouds were like little cotton wool sheep, drifting somewhere on the horizon, but never obscuring the beautiful golden sun.

After a few hours, the terrain changed, and as the coach climbed up a steep, rocky road we realised we were in the mountain region of Yosemite. Sandy and I looked across at one another, held hands and wept silently. A place deep inside had been touched in both of us, moving us beyond words. The majesty of the mountains and the crystal clarity of the air has to be experienced for there are no adequate words to describe the bigness of it all. The energy of the place feels very refined and sacred. No wonder the Native Americans loved their land so much.

The lush greenery and the smell of the pine woods overwhelmed me and I wanted every pore and cell to be soaked in the experience. Our coach party disembarked at the Visitor Centre and we were given a couple of hours to eat lunch and have a look around. Sandy sat on a rock with her sandwiches, looking like a Lion Goddess. I don't know why I thought of that, but she did. I went down to the river. I wanted to splash my face and hair in the cool crystal waters. I paddled for a while, feeling the energy of the mountains and the river soaking into my soul and healing places I didn't know were sore. I waved to Sandy, and she waved back happily from her rock, and for a moment I was transported back to our childhood days by the seaside when time stood still and we didn't have to think or do anything except be happy.

Strangely, later that day, just before we boarded the coach for the next leg of our trip, I noticed that Sandy seemed a little off key and slightly grumpy, and it didn't matter what I did, her dark mood seemed to worsen. Even the uplifting sight of the ancient Sequoia forest didn't smooth the bristles. I dug her in the ribs telling her she was as bristly as a bristlecone pine, but all I got was a black look and silence. By the time we were seated, she was in a black, foul mood. I said something to her and she snapped at me viciously. I was really hurt and couldn't understand why she was feeling that way, but I tried to brush it off and carry on being happy.

Things didn't seem to improve, however, and we assumed a rather prickly and stilted conversational level. It felt like she wanted to kill me if I so much as squeaked, so I just carried on smiling, which seemed to anger her even more, and I chatted to other people instead.

## *Furnace Creek (or the Death Valley Punch Up)*

By the time we got to Death Valley, things had calmed down a little, or so I thought. We travelled through the Mojave Desert until we arrived at our next stopover point, the Furnace Creek Ranch. It wasn't called Furnace Creek for nothing. The air temperature was an unbearable 48° - 50° and even the swimming pool water was the temperature of a very warm bath. That evening, we went out with a few of the friends we had met on the trip, to the restaurant in the Ranch. It was a lovely meal, and we enjoyed the company so much that we carried on to the bar next door. I adore Country Music and I was delighted to find that there was a juke box playing my favourite music in the bar. As Sandy was talking to Jill and Bill and Pat, a family trio we had met on the coach, I slipped off to talk to some people at the bar and was deep in conversation with a young 'cowboy', when Sandy suddenly decided to go back to our chalet. She slapped me spitefully on the backside as she left saying, "I'm off, see you later."

I thought little of it, said, "Goodnight," back at her, and carried on my conversation. The cowboy and I were having a stimulating conversation about the Universe and Life and its mysteries and I felt happy and at peace. He suggested walking me back to the chalet. The warm desert breeze whispered into our faces as the stars, like giant diamonds strewn across a black velvet cloth, twinkled above us. I felt content for the first time in my life and mentally sent out a heartfelt prayer of thanks to Sandy for giving me the gift of this experience and this trip.

# A Work of Heart – Eagles, Deserts, Monkees and Canyons

Our wooden chalet was situated at the edge of the wild and beautiful Mojave desert, famous for spectacular meteor showers or 'shooting stars'. Chet (the young cowboy) and I decided to sit and watch the meteor showers and the shooting stars. We seated ourselves on the soft sand and continued our conversation. The atmosphere was very magical and my companion was a very uplifting, engaging soul. We lost track of time. We also lost count of the shooting stars after about 98, and as we continued our talk about UFOs and life beyond our planet, I looked up at the night sky above us and pointed to what I believed was a UFO. My new friend was more than spooked and confided in me that he had once had a weird encounter with something when he was a small child. As we stared at the stars, we saw a triangular formation of lights right above us. Thinking it was just big, extra shiny stars, I semi-jokingly said, "There it is." At that precise moment, the triangle of lights moved forward slowly then took off at great speed before disappearing into the horizon at warp speed. Chet and I stared at one another, mouths agape in disbelief, and didn't say another word.

In complete synchronicity with weird and wonderful happenings, the very next moment a wild coyote appeared out of the darkness. He stood stock still, staring fixedly at us before he disappeared again into the desert. I couldn't believe what we'd just seen. A wild creature, treating us like we were his special audience. It was one of those moments when the chills run up and down your spine and when you feel you can't explain anything… nor do you need to. You are simply at one with the Universe, the Cosmos and All there Is…

Chet and I continued talking and we both knew that we had shared a unique experience and a rather magical evening. We also knew we would never see one another again but neither of us felt sad about that. I believe that nothing happens by coincidence. The people we meet in our lives are angels in disguise and we are all here for a purpose. The magical part is that we are like comets, trajectories crossing briefly in the galaxy and lighting up the Universe, and each other's lives, when we do. We're not meant to hang on. We are meant to savour the experience, however brief, and let go.

Chet and I decided it was time to say goodnight, realising it must be very late, but not realising it was almost 5:00am and dawn was about to break. We hugged warmly and said goodbye, then I slipped through the chalet doors into the room. What followed shocked me to the core. Sandy leapt out of bed and proceeded to scream and shout, hurling abuse and insults my way like spears. She barely managed to prevent herself from physically attacking me. I didn't know what the hell I'd done wrong. She called me some dreadful names and told me that as far as she spat out the words, "You're on the next plane home, Lady," followed by a rampage of rage that took my breath away.

I was so shocked at this outburst that I shook from head to foot, and then I started to cry. Then I got mad, too. I hated feeling disempowered. I thought she understood that, but obviously not! I launched my own verbal defence and there ensued the most awful row we'd ever had in our lives and I was at the point of packing my bags and leaving, when suddenly Sandy sank down on the edge of the bed. She looked completely beaten. In spite of my dented armour, and fear of a re-launch of the attack, I went over to her and put my arm around her. As I sat down beside her my anger dissipated and I asked her, "Sand, what the hell is all this REALLY about?" At this, she crumpled into a little heap and sobbed like a child in my arms.

"Oh God, I am SO, SO sorry, luvvie… I never meant to say all those things to you. You know I would never hurt you for the world." She could barely speak for crying and it broke my heart. "I am so, so unhappy," she continued. "All this money, all this space, this beauty and this trip are too much for me. I am so homesick and I miss my house but I miss Daddy so much. I have nothing to go home to…"

All the nasty words and the slanging match we'd just experienced suddenly paled into insignificance when I realised she was actually in deep emotional pain. Quite simply, she was letting all her grief for her mum and dad come to the surface. Tiredness and the rawness of not being in familiar surroundings had cracked her shell, at last. She saw me as a butterfly, as someone who could find it easy to be happy wherever I went. Her home was back home, where she'd lived with her mum, dad and sister. The fact that she had to go back to an empty house from our trip where there was nothing and nobody waiting for her was too much to bear. I hugged her tightly and we both cried some more. I told her I loved her with all my heart and nothing would take that away. It crushed me to see her vulnerability for the first time and it touched me to the core. We discussed how we realised that making a big step like our trip could dislodge feelings and emotions that are otherwise stored and left in the box marked 'Pending'. When you are suddenly transported from your comfort zone, and are in an unfamiliar place you feel very insecure and exposed. Sandy had been hanging onto her feelings of rage and despair since Uncle Ted's death. This trip was cathartic for her as well as for me and neither of us had realised it.

The trouble is, when you're close to someone, you don't always see the whole picture. I had my idea of Sandy as the strong, stable one. I thought she saw me as a 'butterfly' and a bit transient! I knew I had many a time envied her home and family life when I was growing up alongside her, but I didn't think she envied me my personality and ability to change and move and be flexible in life.

I resolved to be more attentive and to take better care of her from that moment on.

We sat hugging one another until dawn bathed the desert in golden pink light. Exhausted by the events of the previous evening, we quietly packed our bags ready for the next segment of the trip. We felt we had experienced an emotional volcanic eruption... and we'd survived it because our friendship was made of sterner stuff. Something stronger and deeper had been forged during that long night. And when the dust settled and the sun rose on a new day, our future bonds were already growing and prospering in a more fertile soil.

We would thereafter look at our photographic diary of the trip and fall about in hysterical laughter as we referred to our fallout as the Death Valley Punch Up!

## *Viva Las Vegas!*

Dazzling Las Vegas rose from the desert floor in stark contrast to the peaceful, easy environment of the desert region of Nevada. We were speechless when we saw the mirage that was Vegas appearing from nowhere, and couldn't wait to get to the Las Vegas Hilton where we were staying. En route to the hotel, we stopped off at the Luxor to have lunch. The Luxor, as you may know, is a black glass pyramid that stands like a glittering piece of jet in the desert sand. The entrance walkway is fringed with Egyptian Palms. Magnificent water features cascade into clear pools and the Sphinx guards the entrance. You really do feel you have been transported back in time, and it is actually a surprise to find that the Pharaoh is not in residence!

I will never forget the look on Sandy's face as we went into the dining area and she saw how much food there was to choose from. It was only $11 dollars to eat and drink as much as you wanted. We grabbed our trays and ran around the massive food hall like two people who had never seen food before! When we were stuffed to the gills, we found a little bit of room for a mountain of ice cream topped with every flavour sauce and sprinkles. Good job we didn't have to get straight back onto the coach!

The Hilton Hotel was the epitome of luxury. Our room contained two gigantic beds, a mini-bar filled with more goodies than our local store back home, and the most opulent furnishings you ever saw. Everything was made from white marble! The hotel boasted an awesome swimming pool and after we dumped our cases, we changed into our bathing attire and sashayed out to find a cool spot under the palm trees.

"Sand, I think I've died and gone to Heaven," I sighed. I knew she felt the same way. We languished around the warm, turquoise pool for a little while, before going back to the room to get changed and then we headed out onto the famous 'Strip' to find supper and lose some dollars on the gaming machines.

The lights, sounds and scents were mind-blowing, and everything was so BIG! We walked arm in arm, as our grannies had when they were alive, jaws dropping and eyes widening with every step. We tried our hand at gambling, and the first machine we tried paid out $20!!! We put that aside to pay for supper and continued exploring the Strip, cooing pathetically when we saw the Little White Chapel where Love (and Elvis) Lived and Dreams Came True!

By the time we had wended our weary way back to the Hilton, it was late and we were very tired, but not before we had taken a peek in the Casino did we call it a day and went to bed.

The next morning, I woke in the giant bed to see Sandy kneeling on the giant leather sofa, gazing out of the window across the Nevada desert. Another gentle dawn was just rising and as I joined her on the couch to gaze at the wonder that is Las Vegas, we smiled at each another. There was no need for words. These moments would be immortalized forever in our hearts.

## And on the 6<sup>th</sup> Day...

As Day 6 arrived, I noticed that the days seemed to be running away like wild horses. Today, we were on our way to Zabriski Point, where the film of the same name had been shot a few years earlier. Here, the desert rock formations undulated in great folds, frozen in time. In synchronicity with the unfolding landscape and my thoughts about harmony, a magnificent herd of wild horses galloped in unison, as they raced along in the warm wind. They reflected mine and Sandy's feelings about this vacation.

The incredible rock formations, gullies and mud hills at the edge of the Funeral Mountains, resemble giant waves that undulate across the desert for miles. The light and dark bands in the rock waves stretch for miles like long, creamy strips of toffee. It was and is very hot in this area, due to the sun beating down on the rocks all day with little there for shelter, and we spent a short time taking pictures, before sinking into our seats in the cool, air-conditioned coach once again. From the viewing point of Zabriski, the flat salt plains on the floor of Death Valley are visible in the distance. It is breathtaking.

A day of total contrast greeted us as we climbed the Colorado Plateau into Southern Utah to visit Zion and Bryce Canyon National Parks, otherwise known as Red Rock country. Here, I fulfilled another of my childhood dreams. I took an early evening ride on a tan-coloured horse with a wheat-coloured mane, accompanied by cowboys from the Ruby's Best Western Ranch, out into the canyon. We clip-clopped our way to the canyon through a silent forest of pine trees, stopping awhile to marvel at the tame deer that were chomping on the goodies of the forest floor. Our cowboy guides arranged for us to arrive at the edge of the canyon in time to see the sun setting. Towering mesas and 'salt and pepper' spires and hoodoos graced the canyon floor, millions of years old. Shadows of light and shape changed and moved quickly creating a rainbow of colour and texture as the sun went down. I really wanted Sandy to see this. I took pictures instead, so that at least she could share what I'd seen, albeit second hand.

As I had set off on the trek, Sandy had waved to me, and the love that passed between us was indescribable. It felt like, for a moment, she was the mother I'd always craved, and it felt like I was the daughter she never had. She didn't like horses, but more than that, I knew she wanted me to have my experience alone, because it was my dream, not hers. Another awesome gift she gave me.

When I got back to the chalet, she was in an impish mood. She was sniggering as I was undressing, relishing the thought of a wonderful, cleansing and warming shower. Barely concealing her jollity, she told me to be ready for a surprise. It wasn't 'til I got into the shower that I found the source of her amusement. The surprise was the water. It was bloody freezing cold! She laughed 'til she cried as she heard me dancing around in the stinging cold water, teeth chattering and hollering for a towel!

The Utah climate was similar to that of San Francisco. It is also known as a 'dry state', as it is largely populated with members of the Mormon faith. Sandy was really fed up. She loved her drink! What is it they say? Revenge is a dish best served cold? Well in my case, I got my own back... Revenge is a DRINK not served at all! Tee hee...

## *The Grand Canyon*

A longed for highlight of our trip was the visit to the Grand Canyon. This was something Sandy and I talked about for hours on end when planning our trip. Uncle Ted had loved John Wayne and he and Sandy watched every film he'd ever made. Sandy was so excited because along the route we would be visiting John Ford's Point, a location made famous by the film producer John Ford. *The Duke* starred in many of John Ford's westerns, and this location featured in many of them.

It was also the home of the Navajo Indians – and one of my passions in life was, and still is, Native American culture. Our hotel for the night was situated in the Grand Canyon National Park area, very close to the Grand Canyon. We didn't arrive there 'til early evening, having spent a large part of the day travelling. The first thing we did each day was to find the swimming pool and have a leisurely swim in the cool water to wash away the dust, grime and weariness that had accumulated during the day's travelling.

We had the most amazing woman driving the coach. Her name was Cherie and she was a native of Oregon. Cherie was accompanied by our tour guide, Baron. I spent most of our trip sniggering at Sandy because she developed a crush on him. Alas, her love was unrequited. He was gorgeous, but he was also GAY! I always swore Sandy had a penchant for falling for unobtainable men!

That evening we dined on the most amazing steaks and followed them with pancakes and maple syrup. Nobody can make pancakes the way Americans make them. Exhausted, we fell into bed as the next day we had booked a flight into the Canyon, over Lake Powell and culminating in a visit to the Navajo Reservation to meet the Natives.

I was beside myself with joy. If all my birthdays had come at once, I could not have been happier. Because we were so tired, we opted out of the 5:30 am trip to watch the sun rise over Sunrise Point in the Canyon and some of the party had decided to go on the helicopter trip instead. The tour we chose was the most extensive, as we would be flying over the Lake, landing on the Canyon floor and then taking a jeep ride through the Painted Desert to the Cameron Trading Post, where the Navajo people made and sold their unique silver and turquoise jewellery.

We were transported to the airport on the edge of the Canyon, and I jokingly said to Sandy, "If they think they're taking me up in that butterfly, they're joking!" as we looked out at the tiny airplanes that wouldn't look out of place in your garden! Moments later I was eating my words, as we boarded our particular 'butterfly' and took off on the most exhilarating flight of our lives. Sandy was in the front with the camera, clicking away for all she was worth. I was in the back, looking and feeling very green with motion sickness and could not face looking out of the tiny window of the plane without desiring to part company with my breakfast. I kept it down, however, and I'm glad I did force myself to look outside because Lake Powell is a water world of rocky inlets, its sparkling lakes and deep channels of navy blue and turquoise water resemble turquoise set in stone. Hundreds of tiny yachts and boats were scattered across the extensive lake system like confetti. On the ground, some of the boats were huge, but Lake Powell covers such a vast area that from the air everything appears minute.

We flew over the natural wonder of Rainbow Arch, which is an amazing curved structure formed millions of years ago when the ocean covered the Canyon. The emerald green ribbon of the Colorado River snaked its way along the Canyon far below. Although we didn't see them, the Havasupai people live down there. Our flight lasted for about an hour, and I've never been so happy to see land again. My poor tummy felt dreadful but the warm breeze and fresh air settled me in no time and before we knew it we were climbing into a jeep driven by our Native American tour guide, Howard.

Howard was a BIG man, towering over little Sandy and me. He was a magnificent representative of his people, with the most beautiful, glossy black hair. A raven's wing, caught up in a silver and turquoise clip. I confess, I swooned a little and so did Sandy. 'That look' passed between us and we grinned as we were led to our seats by this lovely man. Howard leaped into the driver's seat, throwing a large black Stetson onto his head then drove us through the beautiful Canyon that was his home. He amused us with a very witty commentary for the whole journey and chuckled to himself as he referred to his assumed Navajo name, 'Iron Man'. No! I didn't fall for it!

We travelled past massive butes and mesas, spires and hoodoos, and marvelled at the fact that this was once the floor of the ocean. It is difficult to relate to such omnipresence from the standpoint of the finite. At times I could feel my head swimming, as if I wanted to faint, and I felt quite dizzy.

We were drawing close to John Ford's Point, when 'Iron Man' Howard stopped the jeep to let us get out and walk around. It was here that I had my most profound experience on the trip so far.

As I walked upon the red ochre coloured earth and gazed in awe at the land around me I had an overwhelming urge to sit cross-legged on the floor of the Canyon. I placed my hands on the ground and felt the earth beneath me and as I looked up to the vast, cobalt blue sky, my heart swelled with love and my hands and body became charged with some kind of energy, and I began to cry. Great heaving sobs were drawn up through my body and I clung to the ground feeling a connection that I've never felt before or since. With all my heart and soul I felt that I had *come home*. I felt my soul and my heart had found their rightful place for the first time in my life and I never wanted to leave, not ever. Sandy came over to me, as she had just had her own emotional experience. While taking photographs 'for Daddy' of the place she and he had seen in the movies, she had been sobbing her dear heart out, too. We hugged one another, again needing no words, and then we just looked at each other's red, dusty, tear-streaked faces and burst into a fit of giggles. Sandy and I used to say that we could never cry 'prettily' like the women on the movies! Our eyes were red and puffy and our noses were all stuffed up, but we got back into the jeep and couldn't stop laughing for the rest of the day!

After looking around at the little stalls filled with beautiful jewellery, we exchanged some light-hearted banter with Howard. I asked him what his Navajo name was and he told me something unpronounceable. When I asked what it meant, he told me it was Navajo for 'Iron Man', but I distinctly caught the twinkle in his piercing black eyes as he said it! Soon, everyone else had made their purchases, so we boarded the jeep and headed back across the Canyon to a place we could have a bite to eat. As Sandy and I wandered around, we could hear haunting music floating across the breeze. I saw a trailer parked a little way across the parking lot, and we headed towards it. Inside was the oldest Navajo Indian I've ever seen. He was beautiful, with long silver hair braided and caught up with brightly coloured beads. His face was leathery and lined and the colour of tanned hide, and there wasn't a space on the face that wasn't wrinkled. Each line was a story in his life as were the notes he was extracting from the instrument he held tenderly in his gnarled old hands. I noticed that his age made him more handsome and dignified, and he exuded a quiet, gentle strength. Something we don't see much in our older people in the Western world. This lovely man was playing this simple flute and the pure, clear notes flew into our hearts and souls like soothing wings of angels. We stood spellbound and in reverence while the man finished his song, then we thanked him for his gift and he bowed graciously without saying a word and we turned and walked away, feeling peaceful and at one with the world

## Day 7

After a good night's sleep and more great food, the coach departed for Scottsdale, Arizona, via the hippy, new-age centred, red rock town of Sedona. It was here that Bell Rock was situated and apparently in the 70's, some guy had sold tickets to a bunch of hippies who believed, as he did, that on a certain day – called something like Harmonics Day – 'Chosen Ones' would be transported to the Pleiades and the collection point was Bell Rock! Can you believe that people actually BOUGHT these tickets? I would have loved to be a fly on the rock when midnight arrived and they were all still sitting cross-legged, 'Ohming', and wondering why no-one had collected them. I also wonder if they got a 'trip cancelled' refund?

We had a fantastic day wandering round all the fascinating bookstores and mystical shops. Sedona is a spiritually oriented town and a lot of people moved there as they believed the area is full of natural vortices, with mystical ley lines converging upon sacred grounds. I believe they are right, but unfortunately the place has become a little too commercialised, and you have to look hard to find genuine mystics and soothsayers among the bandwagon jumpers. That is only my opinion, of course, and it didn't detract from the fact that the place is beautiful and interesting.

We stayed overnight at the Pointe Hilton Hotel, which was absolutely sumptuous and elegant. Sandy and I checked out the massive room with the double, treble, king-sized beds in it, and marvelled at the superiority of the American Service Industry.

Baron, the tour guide, told us that there was a cookout at a ranch in the Sonora Desert, following a trip into the desert to watch the sunset. Did we wish to go? Is the Pope Catholic? Of course we did, and we hurried to get ready for the evening.

I decided that I would get dressed up in my new posh frock and cowboy boots. I was so proud of them. When we were on our way across the Mojave Desert to the Grand Canyon, we stopped over at a place called Denny's Wigwam. It was in the style of an old trading post and once inside, it was like Aladdin's Cave. I headed straight for the boots, hats and jackets area and Sandy followed. As I tried on the prettiest pair of pale blue leather cowboy boots, tipped with silver, I turned to show Sandy and as I turned around, I stopped in my tracks. Sandy was wearing the most incredible jacket I'd ever seen. It was black suede with fringes everywhere and the most exquisite beadwork down the front. She looked stunning in it.

"What do you think? Is it too much?" she asked.

"Jesus, Sand. You look bloody gorgeous. You have to buy it!"

She didn't need telling twice and she snatched the boots from my hand, ran to the counter and paid for both items on her credit card, whispering sidelong, "Sod the expense. There you are duck, we both got a pressie now," she grinned, handing me the bag containing my precious boots. I just hugged her very tightly and my heart swelled with gratitude once again. When we returned home Sandy took pride in wearing her beautiful jacket every time she went into town. She later told me, "I love how people look at my jacket, not my face". Her comments broke my heart. I never saw her as anything *but* beautiful.

We donned our best clothes and went outside to assemble with the others who were going to the cookout. I was so excited. A GENUINE COWBOY COOKOUT IN THE DESERT!

The parking lot was filled with cowboys and cowgirls, dressed to fit the evening, and I fluttered my girly lashes at a Stetson-hatted hunk, whom I later found out was called… Arthur! Arthur told us he had been given an English name by his mother, who was obsessed with England. Arthur was fascinated by our accents but after a while, the novelty wore thin and the spectacle of the early evening Sonora sunset eclipsed everything else.

I cannot believe how many colours there are in one sky. Giant Saguaro Cacti cast their shadows across the ground, their prickly arms reaching up to the heavens in salutation to their magnificent surroundings. Arthur stopped the party to listen and as we all listened, one of our party, Bill, said: "I can't hear anything!"

"Precisely, sir," retorted Arthur, grinning underneath his ridiculous hat. "And if you look to your right, you will see Mother Nature in all her glory," said Arthur, as he instructed us to look at the fiery red sun setting in the Wild Western sky. The sky slowly turned every shade of purple and violet, gold and red, lemon and pink and fluffy clouds streaked with sapphire blue and suffused with gentle pink rays scudded across the vast heavens. It was a natural firework display, finalising in a magnificent desert storm, which arose, seemingly, from nowhere. Warm rain fell in huge droplets, soaking us to the skin in no time at all, and we ran back to the trucks for cover. We watched neon blue forks of lighting as they split the sky and listened to the thunder rolling around like a celestial bass drum.

The party arrived at the Ranch for the cookout. Everywhere there were long trestle tables filled with happy, sunkissed people. In the background the strains of Country Music filled the air, and across the dance floor was a stage where a Hillbilly band were playing. People were dancing the Two-Step and then line dancing took over and the swathes of gingham-clad gals and guys with leather chaps flapping wove in unison across the dirt floor.

We sat down and within a few minutes our waiter arrived. He was a real character, and looked like Doc Holliday from the old western movies. His unruly handlebar moustache was the source of much amusement.

"May I get you something to drink, Ma'am," he mumbled underneath the fuzz. I dug Sandy in the ribs, for she was gawping at this poor man again, and we ordered a few jugs of beer and wine. I have never seen a table so full of food and everyone remarked on the size of the steaks when they were finally served.

A vast wooden plate, that looked like it had been hewn from a giant Sequoia, arrived at the table piled high with what looked like onion rings. Sandy and I filled our plates as we were starving. I asked

'Doc Holliday' when he returned with the beer what the delicious delicacy was…

"Why, that's rattlesnake, Ma'am," he mumbled through his fuzz.

I never realised how green a person could turn until I saw Sandy's face.

"Rattlesnake?" she gulped. "Oh shit, I can't believe I just ate friggin' rattlesnake." She grabbed the jug of beer and quaffed it in one gulp! Not that she needed an excuse. As I said before, she loved her drink!

## *There is no such thing as Death*

Birth, Life and the subsequent Death of the physical form is a process through which all human beings travel. We each have our own way of viewing this process and we each have our own mechanisms for coping with this journey.

When Sandy and I were girls, we would have endless discussions on the Mysteries of the Universe. We always felt that we'd had an agreement that we would incarnate together, and because of this, we also believed we would leave together…

We always had a bond between us, which we both felt very strongly at times, and at others we wished to ignore. Oh, we weren't always roses-round-the-door Pollyanna buddies. We argued a lot, and occasionally ignored one another for days. The longest silence between us was, sadly, to last a couple of years. It was dreadful. I missed her so much and I know she missed me. We were both very stubborn, however. I attempted to get on with my life and she got on with hers. We each had other good and meaningful friends, and I know Sandy had a couple of people in her life she considered to be very special. However, our relationship was unique. It went beyond friendship. It was of the Soul.

After she died, I regressed into a strange state. It was as if I was in a parallel Universe. Everything appeared to be the same. People, places and things were all there as usual but there was a ripping, gaping, tearing wound where my heart used to be. I felt as if there was a black hole in my very soul, and somehow I had to find the strength to just get out of bed in the mornings, to function and exist in this strange, other world. The light had well and truly been extinguished from my life, and I didn't know if it would ever come back again. That is how bad it was for me. I dealt with this by withdrawing from the world in general. I couldn't face working, so I stayed home. Fortunately, at this time, I met Paul who became a long-term partner. I think he must have been sent to me, because it was his love and patience that, in time, helped me through my darkest hours. He was very supportive and without his love and generosity, I don't know how I would have survived.

I spent hours and hours sleeping, and I mean, long hours. I wanted to shut out the world. I wanted to die and go wherever she had gone. I was praying that God would hear my prayers and just take me in the night. But he didn't. I didn't realise that I was suffering a deep depression. I displayed all classic bereavement symptoms, but I didn't know that was what was happening to me. Paul helped me to see that I was grieving. He was a shift worker, which was a great help to me, because he seemed to always be around when I needed him the most. There were days when I'd wait for Paul coming from his late afternoon shift, which meant he didn't get home until 12:30 at night. We would then watch TV into the early hours of the morning, after which I would sleep 'til 4 or 5 o'clock the next afternoon. My days ran into one endless day and in my waking hours, I couldn't deal with normal, everyday activities. It seemed like life had become too much of a chore. I only wanted to be wherever Sandy had gone.

Waking was a nightmare. I had a Morning Monster that lived in the pit of my stomach and for a brief few seconds each day, I could be at Peace. But once MM realised I was awake, it would arise in a black cloud from the depths of my soul and take form... the form was Fear. After Sandy died, my Morning Monster had a field day. It felt like something had gotten hold of my solar plexus, put it in a vice, and was squeezing and gripping it for all it was worth... I couldn't function for at least 2 hours, and the aching loneliness of realising each day that she wasn't coming back was almost too much to bear. And the cold... Sandy had a saying that she used when she was very upset or emotional... she would call me and in a very small voice tell me that 'the ice had come to get her', or 'the ice is back in my heart'. Many a time, I would just listen to her on the phone, in the dead of night, as she would talk about her Cold Monster, and I would try to reassure her I was there for her.

I recall a time when a family rift occurred. This happens with many families from time to time. Sandy was very upset and didn't know what she should do.

Whenever one of us felt that way, we would call the other, and immediately, no matter what the other was doing, we would drop it all and be there for each other, if it was at all possible. Even if it was just to listen.

Well, the ice was with me now. I spent long hours in front of the fire, the heating turned up fully in the house, cocooned in my thick dressing gown. Rarely could I be bothered to dress in day clothes. From time to time, I managed to take a shower or bath. A hot bath gave me sanctuary. They were simply an excuse to go and sob my heart out. I didn't think it was possible to cry that many tears.

Usually, I would be found lying on the sofa with the cats, and the 'poorly blanket'… The poorly blanket was fluffy and soft, the kind you swaddle babies in. It offered some comfort but I was still cold in my soul. I was chilled from the inside and nothing could alleviate this feeling.

The belief systems that had always supported me seemed flimsy now. I was distressed to find that nothing made sense anymore. And so I threw the baby out with the bathwater. Even with the shell of a belief system I felt devastated, bereft and cheated. I did not realise the power of the rage and anger I felt inside. Sandy's death tore me apart, broke me into little pieces and took me to my depths. This was my long, dark night of the soul.

One day, soon after she had passed, I visited the local Spiritualist Church. I don't know why, as I had not needed to do so before, but some part of me felt as if it was wandering in a desert without an oasis in sight. I asked Sandy's friend, who was also her next door neighbour, to go with me. Sandy had been a good friend to her neighbours, and they to her. I know their family felt Sandy's loss very deeply.

We arrived at 7pm, unsure of what to expect, but we were greeted very warmly and led to our seats which were in a circle in the middle of the floor. An assorted bunch had congregated and as I watched more people file in through the door, one particular woman, who was the absolute doppelganger of a lovely lady I had known years previously, struck me. I was so taken aback by the similarity I had to look more than twice to make sure it wasn't Maggie. This lady seated herself about halfway round the circle to my left.

I felt strangely comforted seated there in the warm half light, and as the sitting commenced, Geoff squeezed my hand for reassurance and for some strange reason, he handed me his watch. Sandy had given it to him as a Christmas gift one year, as she always bought her neighbours and their children gifts. That is how generous she was. It meant a lot to them, and the watch meant a lot to Geoff, especially now that Sandy was no longer with us. Geoff and Sheila were always on hand should Sandy need any little jobs done. They were wonderful.

As I recall, at one and the same time, several people announced that they had received the same vision. They described an object that looked like a spider's web, and someone mentioned a piece of turquoise stone in connection with this object. My body tingled from head to foot. I knew without a shadow of doubt what they were talking about. It was a Native American Dream Catcher. Sandy loved them, and she had one above her bed. She had also bought me one when we were in America. She also owned a pair of dream catcher earrings that she loved to wear with her beautiful cowboy jacket bought in Utah. It felt as if something was about to happen. It was a significant sign, but I didn't say anything because I wanted to see what would happen next.

I nearly fell off my chair with shock when suddenly, the lady who reminded me of Maggie focused her attention upon me. "I have a message for you, my dear. Yes, you. The lady in red." That shook me for a start! *Lady in Red* was Aunty Joyce's favourite song and Uncle Ted had dedicated it to her when it was in the charts.

I grabbed Geoff's hand, and I could feel my heart begin to pound. My head swam and I knew with all my heart that my girl had turned up...

Before continuing, the Maggie lady explained to me that she had not intended to visit the church this particular evening. Settled at home, her intention was to curl up by the fire and watch TV. She added that she didn't attend this particular church regularly. She went on to say that she felt she'd been 'dragged out of her chair'. She continued, "I knew with absolute certainty that I had to come here tonight to tell you this," and then she asked me, "Who is Sandra? I have Sandra here, and she says you know her as Sandy." (She used Sandra's birth name, even though most people knew her as Sandy). Overwhelmed, I began to cry. The pain of loss consumed me again and I didn't know what to do. The Maggie lady apologised and asked if I wanted her to continue. I managed to nod my head, saying it was okay. She did not know how much I needed to hear what she had to say.

She told me she had someone with her who was quite young when she had passed over, and whose passing was very recent. She said this young lady had a very strong heart connection with me. She even told me the cause of Sandy's death. It was a DVT in her lung. She went on to describe two other people in detail. I knew without a doubt they were Uncle Ted and Aunt Joyce, Sandy's mum and dad, and she said they sent their love. She also said that the lady (Aunt Joyce) and I had not got on as well as we could have in this life (which was true, as I was the bane of Aunt Joyce's life, for some reason!) She went on to say that this lady loved me very much but couldn't show it, but she wished it to be known that she sent all her love. She also described a deckchair that my Uncle Ted used to sit in on our caravan holidays and his 'garden attire' and bobble hat, and as anyone who knew Uncle Ted will tell you, that was his favourite hat!

She said that Sandy was telling her about a beautiful tropical island, with white sand, turquoise waters and much sunshine... it was Hawaii, where Sand and I concluded our holiday of a lifetime. She also indicated that she was referring to my return trip to the South Pacific, the following Christmas time. The lady said, "She wants you to know she is bringing you sunshine and a huge rainbow and I am getting the song *Somewhere over the Rainbow.*" (Sandy knew I loved *The Wizard of Oz*). I felt this message was giving me hope and telling me to look forward, not back. She said Sandy was very concerned about me, as she knew the extent of my grief... She said this was upsetting her, and I should try to see the sunshine more.

She told me I had to go to the house and look for something, as she hadn't had time to give it to me.

She concluded the reading with the message that Sandy would always be with me, that if ever I needed her, I only had to call and she'd be there, and she was getting a strong message that we were connected by the soul, in fact, we were twins. (Twin Souls). Sandy's dad often referred to us as The Terrible Twins… Sandy was a Gemini, born under the sign of the Twins!

"Oh, she has one last thing to tell you before she goes… she says to tell you she's beautiful now,"… and that brought me to my knees. I knew with absolute certainty that Sand wanted me to know that she no longer had to live inside a body she hated, and that having transcended the physical, she was reconciled with her true nature and true beauty.

The 'twins' part of the message explained why I felt like half of me had been torn away…and I knew with every fibre of my being that this message was true and it was so specific in parts, it could only have been my Sandy saying these things.

I never did go to the house to do a search, as it all got a bit complicated and messy, and anyway, it didn't matter now she'd gone. Material was not important to me. *She* was. I did make one trip to retrieve a few little items that had meant a lot to the pair of us, and I still have the beautiful Christian Reisse Lassen print, *Miracle of Life* in my house. Sandy loved this picture of dolphins, whales and marine life, which she bought at the famed Lassen Gallery in Hawaii.

The first Christmas without her was unbearable. I tried my best to deal with it by closing down all systems, but Sandy wouldn't let me, not completely. Just a few days before, I had received, in the post, the most beautiful calendar from Geoff and Sheila, Sandy's old neighbours. Geoff had written a little note to explain that he'd found this in a market and had the strongest urge to get it and send it to me. The calendar was illustrated with a breathtaking array of Christian Lassen pictures!

Thereafter, I began to realise that Sandy was still around. What follows is an account of some of the Sandy Miracles, as I call them. All are authentic and as accurate as I can recall.

# The Eagles Miracle, (Friday 15<sup>th</sup> June 2001) - My Birthday Gift

My birthday is on 20<sup>th</sup> April. Sandy's was 31<sup>st</sup> May. For our 40<sup>th</sup> birthdays, Sandy threw a party - a double celebration. She knew I didn't have any spare cash, and it was her way of giving me a gift to remember our joint milestone. She hired a venue, disco and caterers and it all went with a bang! We invited lots of our friends and they came from far and wide to help us celebrate the Big 4-0!

Sandy never forgot my special day, and she always sent me the most beautiful cards. I still have the last one she ever sent me. It goes on display each year, its message is timeless and so typically Sandy. She also made sure I had a lovely gift each birthday. I wish I had her 'presence' instead of her presents...

After she went, Paul took over her 'job' and there would be something special from him, and something he'd found to give me, assisted by the voice of Sandy, deep in his heart.

20<sup>th</sup> April 2001 is a day I'll never forget. Paul found Sandy's card and put it on the mantelpiece, and as I came downstairs to my 45<sup>th</sup> birthday, I was greeted with more cards and presents and a big warm hug. As I opened my cards, and looked at the things Paul had bought for me, I heard a familiar voice telling me, "I can't give you MY 'presence', but there IS another present on its way to you, from me, but you'll have to wait a bit and be patient." I had this feeling in my tummy of utter excitement and I could almost see her face in front of me, beaming her special excited smile.

A few minutes later, Paul said to me, "Erm... I have something else for you, but you'll have to wait a bit, as I've had to order it, and it's a surprise!" I nearly fell off the chair! Six weeks later, I got the Gift of a Lifetime, once again, from Sandy, through Paul.

One day, two weeks prior to the surprise, Paul called me at work and insisted that I ask my employer for a half day off. "You have to get the afternoon of Friday 15<sup>th</sup> June off, and you have to leave at 12 noon. I won't take no for an answer. In fact if you don't ask him, I'm going to ring him myself. Jools, it's really important, just trust me and do it." I wasn't sure I'd be able to do it, but thankfully, my boss agreed and I booked the afternoon off. I was intrigued, but decided to trust Paul, as he'd never let me down before and I knew it must be very important if he was this insistent.

Friday 15<sup>th</sup> June arrived, and as agreed, I left work at the stroke of noon and headed home. I had strict instructions to go straight home where Paul would join me, as he had to take time off work as well. This was not an easy thing to organise, as he works shifts and had to arrange for cover. I learned later that he had (with the stealth of the SAS) been working on this surprise for some time.

I hadn't a clue what to wear, because I didn't know where we were going. Paul told me to wear smart casual, so I dressed in a good pair of jeans, a smart top and a denim jacket and we jumped into the car and drove off. Paul didn't give me any indication or clue whatever of what lay ahead.

I had such an excited feeling in my tummy, and strangely enough, I could feel Sandy's presence all around me. It felt as if she was excited too, for some reason. I never once thought about the birthday surprise thing, although with hindsight, it should have been obvious. All morning at work, I had been humming a Sandy song, and it was only later that the pieces fell into place, making a beautiful picture.

We set off at precisely 12:45pm and drove for miles, down country lanes and winding roads. I hadn't a clue where we were, let alone where we were going. Paul was not going to tell me, either. About two and a half hours into the journey, and on a country road in the middle of nowhere, I remarked to Paul, "Well, will you look at that? That pub over there is called The Eagles!" It was significant to me, only because of Sandy and our connection.

In due course, we arrived in the centre of Birmingham. I still hadn't the faintest idea what was going on. I saw a sign for a Sea Life Centre, and as we'd discussed the possibility of going to a Sea Life Centre nearby to swim with and feed the sharks. I thought Paul had decided to take me for a surprise swim! The only fly in the ointment being that it was now past closing time.

I'd never been to Birmingham so I didn't know that the car park of the huge building we pulled into was the National Indoor Arena. Paul remained silent, grinning at me now and again and squeezing my hand. I still cannot believe I had not a single clue as to the outcome of this journey. Paul told me we had to park here, because we were going for a meal and he'd been advised to park in this car park as all the others would be busy... and I believed him! As he went to get a parking ticket, I sat in the car, and started humming the song I'd been humming that morning, and Sandy's energy jumped into the car and into my heart... For some unknown reason, I felt tears pricking my eyes and I swear to God, it felt like she'd squeezed my hand. I began to feel something else in my gut. Anticipation, mixed with a little fear and trepidation...

Paul opened the door and helped me out of the car. We climbed the steps of this massive building and I continued to question him, trying to extract the surprise. Abruptly, he stopped walking and turned to me and as I looked past his shoulder, there on the wall behind him was a poster. A poster advertising a concert. THE EAGLES IN CONCERT. I felt faint and my voice shrank as I said to him, "Oh my God, is that why we're here?"

"Yes, my darling, it is. Unless of course you would rather go someplace else?"

My legs were like jelly and I croaked, "Is it the *real* Eagles?" Paul fell about laughing, hugging me and telling me, yes, it *was* the *real* Eagles! It was not a tribute band, but the *real live* Eagles.

I crumpled like a 5-year old and cried like a baby.

Paul explained that this was the surprise he'd promised me 6 weeks earlier, and that it was a joint gift from Sandy and him. He later explained the complicated process that led to the gift, and once again, I felt the joyful co-creation between a departed soul and a living angel!

To say that the concert was one of the highlights of my life is an understatement. Sandy's presence was so strong it was as if she was in the seat next to me. The band was sensational and even Paul, who didn't particularly like the Eagles, said it was the best live concert he'd ever attended. I didn't stop crying all night!

As the three hour long concert drew to a close, I was aware that I had been holding my breath for one particular song... I prayed and prayed that they would play it, but the end of the concert came all too soon, and the one song I prayed for hadn't been sung. The experience had been the best experience in ages, and had lifted my spirits so high, I felt I was flying. The band performed a couple of encores to rapturous standing ovation, and then they left the stage. The audience were not giving up that easily, and suddenly, as the band burst onto the stage for their third and final encore, my song crashed into the air like a thousand angel wings and I broke down and sobbed from my boots as they played the one song I had been humming all day... *Take It Easy*!!! I felt Sandy leap into the air with my heart, and if I never see another band live again, that experience and that gift was the best ever. It was truly Sandy's Presence!!!

# Pictures from the Past

*My beautiful mum, Evelyn and very handsome dad, Roland, on their wedding day in 1955. The cake was real!*

*Sandy's lovely Nana and Grandad, Aunt Doll and Uncle Bill in their back garden. Aunt Doll was Aunty Joyce's mum and my gran's sister. The factory of the Liverine Pet Food Manufacturer (seen behind them) ran the length of Fraser Street and everybody's back gardens on this side of the street were privy to this austere backdrop. Quite a number of Grimsby folk were employed there for many years. My most vivid memory of the factory was the pungent aroma of aniseed that pervaded the air for years. At 8.30 every morning the factory hooter would summon the workers, who could be seen teeming down the street and clattering down the cobbled entrance to the main gate. At 5.00 pm it all happened again and my friend Debra and I would sit on Gran's front gate saying 'night night' to them all. It was like Willy Wonka's but without the chocolate! The Liverine is sadly no longer there.*

*Sisters, sisters, there were never such devoted sisters' (or as my Uncle Ted referred to them - The Tiller Girls). From left to right: Back row - Aunt Doll (Sandy's gran) in her slippers, aww bless… Aunty Nora (the one that ran away to the Nottingham Goose Fair) Aunt Renee (pronounced Rennie). Front row – Aunt Marian and Elsie (my gran). Apart from Aunt Nora (the Nottingham renegade) they were all born and then lived in the same street all their lives. What an achievement by today's standards!*

*Taken in the late 1940's here are the sisters again at a family wedding. The only time the family had a get-together, according to Uncle Ted, was at 'hatches, matches and dispatches'. L to R: Emily, Doll (Sandy's nana), Elsie (my gran), Marian, Renee and Nora. My Uncle George, after a few beers at granny's wake, was heard to remark about this picture, 'Well, they must have had good personalities, cos there ain't a bonny bugger among 'em.' Quite!*

*My handsome Uncle Ted, Sandy's dad. Sadly, it is the only picture I have of him. It was taken around Christmas 1980.*

*Aunty Joyce and my beautiful baby boy, Jamie.*

*Sandy and her beloved 'Freddie'. This was the car she and Uncle Ted had driven between them, prior to his passing. Sandy loved this little car and loved nothing more than to wash and shine her baby.*

*Fred, a dear friend of ours from Texas and Sandy. We were all going out dancing and Sandy was beside herself - just like her mum before her, she went ga-ga in the presence of anyone with a 'Yankee' accent!*

*1995 in Chicago's (an American style restaurant - no longer there) where Sandy and Jay took Fred from Texas, so he'd feel more at home! Oh dear... those waistcoats!*

> *Would you
> like to know
> what I would wish
> for you,
> if I could have
> any wish
> I wanted?*

Blue Mountain Arts

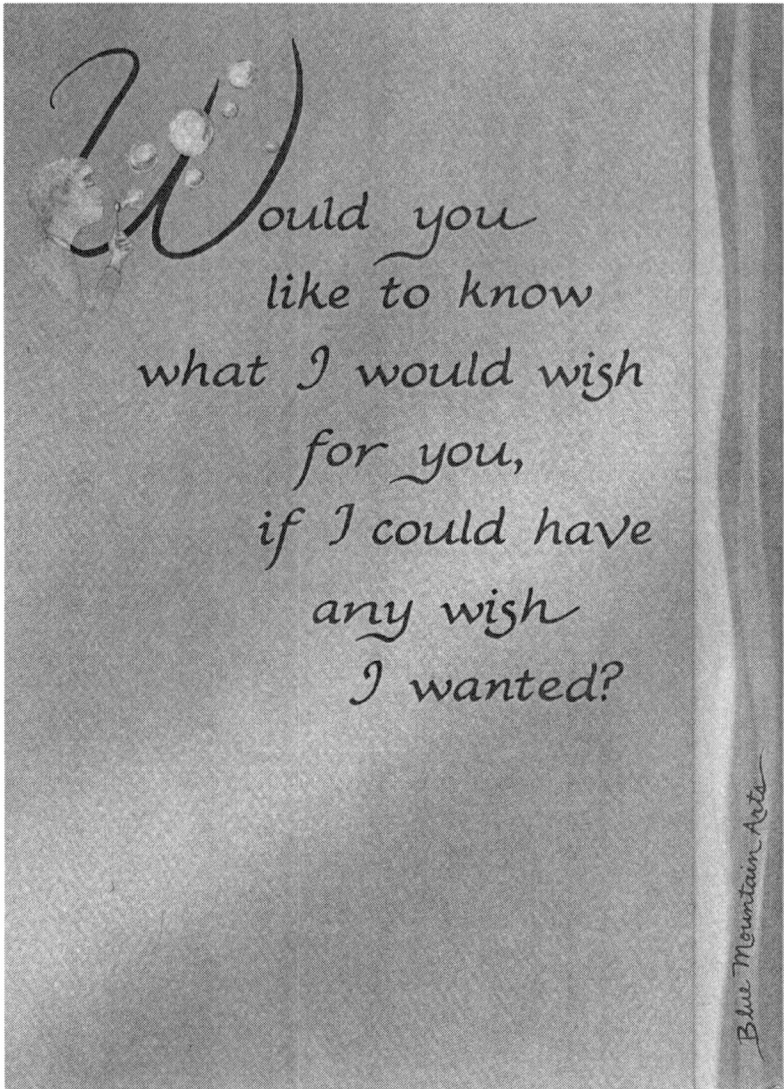

*This is the last card she ever sent me...*

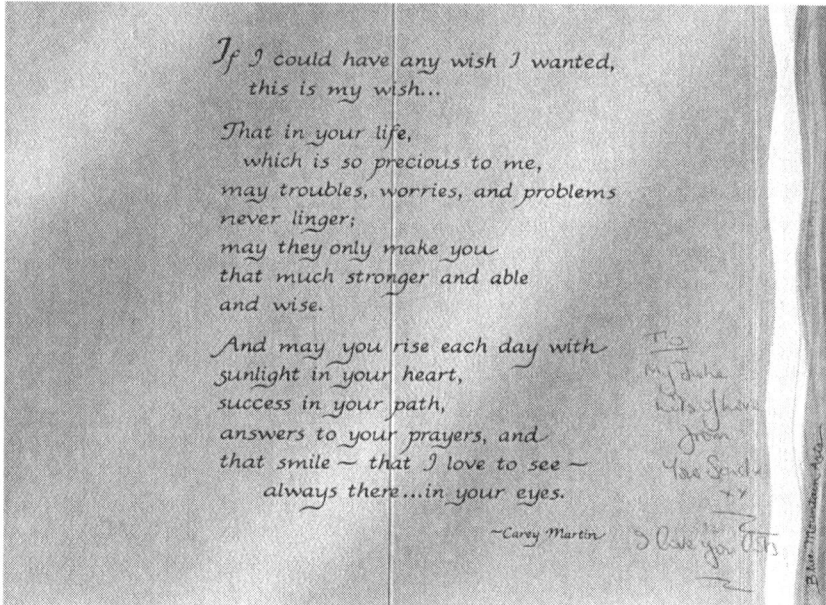

> *If I could have any wish I wanted,*
> *this is my wish...*
>
> *That in your life,*
> *which is so precious to me,*
> *may troubles, worries, and problems*
> *never linger;*
> *may they only make you*
> *that much stronger and able*
> *and wise.*
>
> *And may you rise each day with*
> *sunlight in your heart,*
> *success in your path,*
> *answers to your prayers, and*
> *that smile — that I love to see —*
> *always there...in your eyes.*
>
> —Carey Martin

*I treasure it because it is the essence of her beautiful and loving nature. The writing is as clear as if it was done yesterday.*

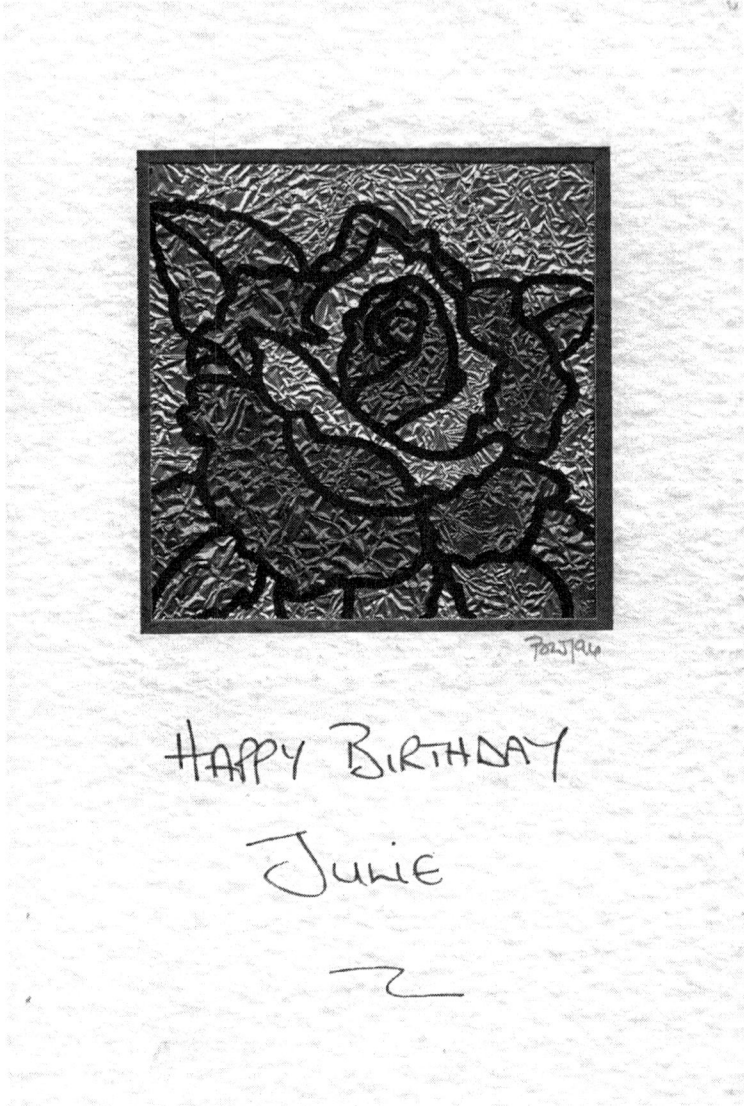

*My last ever birthday card from Sandy, just three months before she went out of my life…*

To My Julie,

lots of love
&

Have a happy day sweetie

Sandy xxx
☺

I don't know what
I've done to deserve you, but
I thank God we were sent
together! Sand.

*Los Angeles LAX Airport Hotel 1996 - We were mooching around the airport hotel, awaiting the call for our flight home from our amazing holiday and when we discovered this bunch of cowboys checking in. Not one to miss a trick, Sandy collared them for a photo shoot. Yeehaw!*

*1996 - That big hole in the ground! Me and the gal in the Painted Desert, Grand Canyon, Arizona… picture taken by Howard 'Iron Man', our Navajo tour guide. Obviously exercising his artistic licence*

*The Painted Desert, Grand Canyon, Arizona Howard, our Navajo tour guide, and I discussing his trailer. I was gutted that he didn't live in a tipi, like his ancestors. He found this highly amusing and kept calling me 'Julie Yellowhair' and asked if I knew Princess Diana?*

*Aloha Hawaii! Sandy and I sitting in the bar of the Outrigger Malia Hotel in Waikiki, waiting for Arnold's Karaoke to strike up! After this picture we did a mean duet, singing one of our favourite songs, Take it Easy by the Eagles*

*Los Angeles Police Department. Only she could hijack a couple of hunky cops and not get arrested! This was taken in a busy evening street in L.A. These unsuspecting guys had stopped at the red light and Sandy dashed over spotting a photo opportunity*

*It's MARGARITA TIME! Every day whilst in America, Sandy and I toasted 'absent friends' with the local version of a Margarita. It became our favourite holiday tipple. These two were by far the best - look at the size of those glasses! Not content with just one, she set about supping mine as well! Nowadays, I toast my absent friend with our special cocktail...*

*Aloha and Maholo, my Sand!*

## *The Clangers, Paul and the Sandy Card*

Before I tell you about this little miracle, I have to explain that one of Sandy's and my favourite programmes, when we were kids, was *The Clangers*. We would watch it together, and then pretend to be the Clanger mice, visiting the Soup Dragon behind her mum's couch! Sand loved Tiny Clanger best. To my heartstopping delight, my friend Anne surprised me on my birthday with a soft toy version of Tiny Clanger, who made the Clanger whistling noise when you pressed her tummy. It made me cry. Thank you, Anne! I just wished someone had made them 5 years earlier!

31st May, 2000 dawned, and with it my usual sadness and heavy cloud of grief. I tried so hard to be positive, but Sandy's birthday is never easy. I find that for days before the date, I get paranoid about people dying, and it's usually Paul who reminds me that my subconscious is anxious and remembering my girl.

It was late at night, on 30th May and, unknown to Paul, I had been to the shop to buy a birthday card for Sandy. I don't know why, but I didn't tell him I'd done it, because I thought he might think I was being silly. God knows why, because he had never ever given me that impression... however, it helped me to see and know about the miracle which was about to occur. Buying a card for a dead person might be someone else's idea of crazy, but it helped me to feel closer to her if I could still do this one small thing and with Paul in the next room, busily engaged in some computer work, I quietly wrote onto the card the following message :

*Happy Birthday to my Tiny Clanger, wishing you all the love in the world, and hoping you are with your Soup Dragon watching over me... I Love You... Your Jool xxxxxxxxx*

At the precise same moment, I heard Tiny Clanger whistling from the next room. Paul had spotted my little friend sitting atop the computer, and for some strange and inexplicable reason, 'just felt to give it a squeeze'.

I called through to him to ask what he was doing. "Aah, Tiny Clanger is just saying 'hello'," said Paul.

I started to cry. Paul came through, worried that he'd upset me in some way. When I explained that I had just put down the pen from writing my birthday message to Sand, he hugged me and said, "Well, I guess that was Sand again, letting you know she has got her card."

## Tequila Sunrise – a Message for a Friend in Need

I had been talking to a dear friend one morning on the phone. We were discussing, of all things, alcohol and drink related problems. As I put down the phone, I heard the song *Tequila Sunrise* come onto the radio, and at that point I felt Sandy's energy. She was telling me to tell my beautiful friend that drinking was not the answer, and that even after you'd tried to blot it all out, you still had to carry on the next day – only with a hangover! I was using the land line for the internet connection at the time, to do some research for this book, so I decided to send my friend a text message instead. At the exact time I started to tap in the message, all the power in the house went out. Everything, including the computer, went off. I panicked as I hadn't thought to back up my work prior to going to the mobile phone, and thought I'd lost at least a page. The power came back on almost a few seconds later, and to my utter surprise and delight, I hadn't lost any work… I felt that Sandy had been reinforcing my decision to talk to my friend, and having had drink problems herself, she knew firsthand how futile alcohol, as a prop, is!

*NB – to date, my friend is as beautiful as she ever was, and is a successful and brilliant counsellor and gifted psychic.

## My Train Dream – Harry Potter and Platform Nine and Three Quarters

I am sure my personal hero JK Rowling won't mind my reference to her own work of the heart, *Harry Potter*, as it is of significance to my train dreams. They do say that life imitates art, and vice-versa and the brilliant idea that we can depart for another world, a parallel world, from a platform that is actually only seen by those needing to take the journey, is how I see 'death'. Aunt Joyce, Uncle Ted and Sandy all departed on the same train, from the same platform in my dream prior to their departure from the world in which I still exist. Only since I began to see and feel the thinning of the veil did I realise this simple truth. Like the Muggles in *Harry Potter*, we go through life oblivious to that which is not under our very noses. We tune out, rather than tune into the many frequencies of vibrational matter that surround us, because we don't always need to be operating on many wavelengths at the same time. Only when something like physical death occurs are we kick-started into wanting answers to questions about Life and Death. These radio stations are not only open to mystics and psychics. Anyone on this planet has the equipment and ability to tune in, if they wish to. You only have to stop, be still and listen to your heart.

*Quote: The distance between Life and Death is like a Fine Blue Line (Nick and Jo Davey and Gina O'Brien).*

We are a radio audience, and we can choose to tune into which ever radio station we want to listen to. I had this picture of an old battered wireless, the kind my Uncle Ted kept in his garage. It was an old Bush model, I believe. As more mature readers will recall, these primitive music centres were a bit hit and miss. On the radio was a large plastic wheel, and along the front of the display bit of the radio was a line of numbers. Radio frequency numbers. There were three wavebands; MW, LW and SW (medium, short and longwave). The longwave stuff was for listening to obscure Swedish and Nordic stations, and long range weather forecasts. Medium and shortwave stations could be more easily picked up because the stations were not so far away. You operated it with an on/off switch and a tuning dial.

Before you managed to lock onto a frequency that was broadcasting something audible, there was usually a lot of interference, fuzziness and whistling. You could be forgiven for thinking you'd contacted aliens, such was the interference at times.

# I am There

Bear with me while I digress for a moment. But I find I am inspired to insert here the following poem. I gave Sandy a copy after her dad died and it has been very comforting to me. As I wrote the title, I realised my error, and moved to correct it. Then I was nudged from Sandy, who is ever-present to remind me of another message from her, reassuring me she would be here, helping me to write this book. Nothing happens by coincidence!

### I AM NOT THERE...

*Do not stand at my grave and weep.*

*I am not there. I do not sleep.*

*I am a thousand winds that blow.*

*I am the diamond glints on snow.*

*I am the sun on ripened grain.*

*I am the gentle autumn rain.*

*When you wake in the morning's hush,*

*I am the swift uplifting rush*

*of quiet birds in circling flight.*

*I am the stars that shine at night.*

*Do not stand at my grave and cry.*

*I am not there. I did not die.*

## *Sandy's Christmas – How it 'Snowballed' from a Tree*

For many reasons, I gave up 'doing' Christmas a long time ago. I realised the symptoms of Christmasphobia were not getting any better as the years went by, and by September in any given year, I was beginning to experience panic attacks whenever I thought of Christmas, heard advertisements on the TV or radio and worst of all, began seeing decorations and merchandise appearing in the shops three months too early. I am not religious, so I didn't have a religion to do it for. I am not an atheist, or a Jehovah's Witness, so I couldn't use my religion as an excuse not to do it. I decided I was going to 'drop out' Christmas from my life. I realised I had begun to hate Christmas and what it had become. My childhood memories were sad ones; many were tinged with sadness, because Christmas in our house was an excuse to eat, drink and make a nuisance of yourself! Without exception, my mother and father falling out in lumps, and my father over-drinking would spoil our family Christmases. I don't feel that misery and despair should be part of the Season of Goodwill.

The best part of any Christmas I can recall is centred around a Sandy memory. As kids, weeks before the festive season began, we would rendezvous to 'talk about Christmas'. We'd climb into bed or Uncle Ted's Ford Anglia and wrap the travel rug around us, then we'd talk for hours about what we loved best… mine was always about a fantasy Christmas, where all the family was happy, Dad was in a great mood and more importantly, sober! Mum was content to cook and smile a lot. The house would be filled with love and we children would open our presents in an atmosphere of innocence and joy. Sandy and I would recall Christmases past and all the presents we'd had, and we'd talk about what we wanted in our sacks this year. During those talks, I felt happy and almost sedated, as I did whenever I was around at Sandy's house. It was safe there. You could be a kid again.

In complete contrast to me, Sandy absolutely loved Christmas. She had only happy memories of times gone by, and by all accounts, her mum and dad tried to make it a magical time for all.

One of my biggest regrets is that I didn't get to spend her last Christmas on Earth with her. I had flown to the Marshall Islands via Hawaii to spend a month on a tropical island next to a lagoon. In view of my view of Christmas, I didn't need much persuading when a handsome USAKA Sergeant called John invited me on vacation. We had met on Sandy's and my last night in Hawaii and he was very charming. Some would say I was crazy to fly halfway around the world to spend a month with a man I'd only just met, but it felt right. It also felt good. I adored the U.S. and the chance to be in Hawaii again might never be repeated.

Whilst I was on the beautiful tropical island of Kwajalein, swimming in crystal oceans and eating breakfast by the lagoon watching the Pacific dolphins leaping for joy, my Sandy was back home in freezing cold England. She had been to see me prior to my departure and had given me a wad of dollars that were left over from our summer trip.

I was so excited about my adventure that I never gave a thought to the fact she would be home alone. If only... She waved me off and said smiling, "Ring me on Christmas Day," and her little flower-dressed figure drove away,

I did call her on Christmas Day and she was happy to speak to both John and me. She secretly fancied John, I later found out. He was a John Wayne fanatic, a passion they both shared. On New Year's Eve, I called her again but there was no answer. I tried the next day and found she had gone to bed early, as New Year was just too painful for her. It was worth the hangover she was nursing, apparently.

It should have been Sandy who visited with John, really. They would have gotten along really well. He turned out not to be Mr Right for me; rather he was Mr Right Now. I had a long way to go and a lot of frogs to kiss before my Prince Charming appeared for me!

I digress. It wasn't easy saying, "I don't do Christmas." That statement gets a mixed reaction, but not many people would accept my decision. I found myself justifying my actions and resented it after a while. Every time I heard someone moaning about the stress, expense, hassle, etc., I asked them why they were doing it to themselves.

"Because it's Christmas, and you do, don't you? Besides, we have to. It's the kids. If it wasn't for the kids..." blah-de-blah. I've heard it all.

When I met Paul, I was so happy to find him feeling as I did about it. We enjoyed *not* doing Christmas the first year we were together. He was working on Christmas and New Year's Eve anyway, so that someone with a family could have the chance to be at home. We enjoyed a lunch of beans on toast, followed by a light supper. Paul drank alcohol at that time, from which he now abstains. So, while he enjoyed a few beers, I had a medicinal shot of brandy, and we were happy with that. We didn't mind that we didn't have any visitors, people who knew us knew our views and had become used to the idea that we were not going to reciprocate cards, gifts, etc. I simply didn't want to participate in anything that wasn't in my heart. That was really important to me.

The following year we did the same thing, and by our third year together, my bereavement process was well underway. I later realised that banning Christmas was my way of protecting my emotions.

Prior to Sandy's death, she would always invite me to stay with her for Christmas and it drove me crazy. She absolutely loved it, and I absolutely hated it, but I knew it was important for her that I was around, because of her own loss. Her first Christmas without Uncle Ted she spent with strangers, because she couldn't bear to be in the house without him.

It felt important that Sandy's subsequent Christmas alone should be a happy occasion and so on Christmas Eve, I arrived at 26 Southfield Avenue, armed with my nightie, slippers, toothbrush and the customary gifts.

After she had passed, I learned the significance of giving not only your presents, but more importantly, your Presence. It hurt deeply when I realised Sandy's physical presence was absent. It broke my heart, which remained broken for some years to come.

On this occasion, bless her wonderful heart, she'd gone to town. Tree, lights, tinsel, decorations, drinks, food, nuts and nibbles, you name it, it was there. Presents were scattered under the tree and she'd redecorated the house. When I walked up the driveway of my second home (sometimes, it felt like my only home) her smiling face at the window melted my heart. She was so childlike at times and as excited as it was possible to be. Nat King Cole crooned through her new music system (a definite upgrade on the old Dansette) and she was singing and dancing in the window oblivious to passersby. I was greeted with a crushing hug and an oversized glass of wine. Christmas had begun.

Her planned agenda was to have tea, then take a walk to the pub where she and her dad used to go. I didn't really feel like it, but I went anyway. She expressed a wish to attend the midnight service at the local church, and in spite of my tiredness, I agreed to go. It was a strange night, because once we were in the pub, Sandy made an uncharacteristic play for a handsome stranger who was standing at the bar, minding his own business. She drank steadily and became more inebriated. She then invited the stranger to accompany us to church.

St Giles is a picturesque little church in the parish of Scartho, where Sandy and I grew up, and it was popular for family 'hatches, matches and dispatches'. The church held many memories for both of us, and it was fitting that we spent Christmas Eve in this candlelit sanctuary.

At about 11:30pm, Andy, no longer a stranger, and I were chatting when we realised Sandy had gone missing. She had been gone for about 10 – 15 minutes, when we realised she was not in the powder room nor was she in the pub. We searched everywhere and our search became more frantic as we realised that it was freezing cold outside and she was very drunk. Then, in a flash of inspiration on this cold and frosty, starry Christmas card night, I knew where she would be.

Andy and I hurried to the church, just around the corner from the pub, and as we raced up the icy path, we could hear the organ playing and the congregation singing *Away in a Manger*. Pushing open the heavy door and creeping inside, I scanned the crowd. Tucked neatly in the back row huddled against the wall, was my girl. She was crying quietly into her handkerchief and I pushed past people to get to her and give her a hug. I had no inkling of the depth of her grief... I do now.

*Away in a Manger* was Uncle Ted's favourite hymn. He also loved *All Things Bright and Beautiful*, but this was his Christmas song.

The pain of loss was simply too great for Sandy to bear, and she could not contain her outpouring of grief. People began to look around and some began tut-tutting and shaking their heads, which angered me. Call themselves Christians? Season of Goodwill? Bah, Humbug!

Andy, bless the man, came to help me with Sandy. I knew that I had to get her outside and into the fresh air. I persuaded her to follow me, and slowly we picked our way outside. Frost sparkled on the ground. Above us a canopy of stars twinkled in the night sky. I showed her the Christmas Star, wrapping my arms around her and letting her grieve. I rocked her gently and told her that daddy was sitting on the Christmas Star, watching over us. We stayed there until the congregation had departed. The lovely vicar came across to check that Sandy was okay. I didn't realise it, but he knew the family, had conducted Aunt Joyce and Uncle Ted's funeral services, and he was very comforting and gentle. His presence, therefore, was invaluable and greatly appreciated.

Andy and I each took an arm and, gradually, this strange trio hobbled home. Sandy picked up, buoyed up by alcohol and the release of her pent up emotions and she began dancing and singing very loudly. By the time we reached home, she was feeling well enough to launch herself at poor Andy again. Thankfully, he and I managed to manhandle her into bed, fully dressed after which she fell into a coma and Andy departed discreetly.

Christmas morning she didn't even have a headache! We opened our presents, giggling like two little girls. We knew we were attempting to relive former Christmases but it didn't matter that they were not quite the same. What mattered was that we tried and that we were together. This difficult period of her life, was helped by regular intake of alcohol and lots of sleep. We shuffled through the next couple of days before I went home. I was well ready for my own space.

Solitude had never been a problem for me. I was happiest when on my own. In contrast, Sandy knew the peace and warmth of a family unit that offered safety and comfort. That was a fundamental difference in our lives, but these differences only served to enhance our relationship.

It was a cold November in 1999. Christmas was fast approaching. Everyone was rushing around as usual, and tensions were mounting everywhere. I was glad to get home in the evening. One evening, for no reason at all, I was thinking about Sandy. Nothing new there. I asked Paul if he thought it might be okay if I just bought a little something for Sandy, seeing as how she had loved this time of year. It was in the same spirit as buying a birthday card and flowers on her birthday and he didn't see anything wrong with that.

Then came the weekend that changed our lives in a beautiful way. It was a Christmas Miracle. Paul had gone to work. There were only a few days to go 'til Christmas Eve. I was staring at the space where the bay window was situated, when the most wonderful peace washed over me and a dreamy, other-worldly calm presided. As if in a trance, I decided to go out and look for a poinsettia that I could put in the window. Sandy adored the colour red, and it felt right, so off I set in search of a suitable plant. With little awareness of how I'd arrived there, I found myself in Scartho village, and drew up outside Gambles the Florist, the little shop that sold plants and groceries. Sandy and I had walked to this lovely old shop many times in our lives. I hadn't felt so peaceful and happy in a long while, and as I looked around the displays out on the pavement, the most beautiful and perfect Christmas tree caught my eye. It seemed to shine as if lit by unseen fairy lights. Drawn to it like a magnet, I gently picked up the little tree and put it in the back of the car, then went inside to pay for it.

Okay, it was a larger plant than I'd planned to buy but what the heck? Now what? The gentle energy in my gut guided me back to the car and it seemed the most natural thing in the world to visit the local garden centre for something with which to dress my lovely little tree.

I floated around the Christmas department, feeling the love of Sandy in my heart, and choosing the brightest, most sparkling baubles I could find. I felt like a kid in a sweet shop and before long I had filled my basket with shiny tinsel, tree chocolates and candy canes. Only one more thing, then home.

Taking my overflowing bags back to the car, I was bubbling with good will. This must have been how Sandy felt. I was shaking by the time I arrived back home. Partly I was afraid of Paul's reaction, so I decided to keep the tree a secret for a little while longer.

Paul departed for his late afternoon shift, which meant he would be home around 11pm so I had a few hours to get things set up. I fired up the music centre and, together, the Eagles and I dressed the little Christmas tree in all its glory. I stepped back to admire my handiwork, and before I switched on the twinkling fairy lights, I filled my glass with brandy. Raising my glass to my darling girl, my eyes shining with tears, I whispered, "Merry Christmas, Sand. This is from me to you," and the room filled with the warm red glow of two thousand years of Peace and Goodwill to all Men…

The fire glowed in the grate and I sat nursing my brandy for some time, taking an occasional sip and revelling in feeling amazing. And in that timeless place, Sandy spoke to me.

"Thank you, my Jewel. You don't know what this means to me. You see, I knew if you could find Christmas in your heart you would begin to heal your pain. And you have taken the first big step and I'm so proud of you. Christmas is from the heart, not from the credit card. Have fun, my angel and know that I'm always with you and always will be."

Paul arrived home at around 11:30pm and as he walked into the sitting room he dropped his bag on the floor and stared. He looked at me, and tears filled his eyes. I thought I'd upset him, but then he walked over to me and hugged me tight.

"Thank you, Jool. Thank you," he cried. Great gulping sobs wracked his body, and we cried together.

"Is this okay with you?" I asked tentatively.

"Oh God, darling… you have no idea. When I walked into this room, it was as if the years fell away from me and I was a little boy again. This is the kind of Christmas I used to dream about." It would seem that healing had taken place for both of us.

A couple of days later, I was preparing dinner when Paul walked into the house bearing a gift. He set the pretty package on the table, gave me a quick kiss and said, "Well, go on then. Open it!"

I carefully eased apart the delicate wrapping paper. Amid the soft white tissue lay the most beautiful little Angel I'd ever seen. She was dressed in a soft, white raggy doll dress, with tiny shoes on her feet that had gold stars on and in her tiny hand was a wand with a golden star on the end. Her hair was made of wool and on her head she wore a little golden crown made from stars. Unlike any other angels, she looked just like Sandy. I held her to my heart, tears rolling down my face, and Paul said, "Happy Christmas, darling. The little tree needed a Sandy Angel, didn't it?"

Paul later told me that he had been walking past a little arts and crafts shop up the road from our house, when Sandy called him inside! She took him to the display at the back of the shop, where the little raggy doll angel lay. To this day, my Sandy Angel graces the tree at Christmas. Thank you Sandy. Thank you Paul.

# Owl Magic

I was driving home one night, having had a bad day at work, stressed and feeling lonely and depressed. I had just found out that a beautiful lady, whom I had met through an esoteric website, had passed away. It was totally unexpected, just like Sandy, and because she had become a heart friend in a short space of time, even though I never met her, she mattered to me very much. She had just moved house with all her family, and was very excited about living on the edge of the Arizona desert… when I learned of her demise, my heart contracted and my stomach squeezed but as I was at work, I had to hold it all in.

The pain of Sandy came crashing back to me, like a tidal wave, and once I got in the car, I began to cry, deep, racking sobs. Suddenly, out of nowhere, on a busy dual carriageway of the A180, the most amazing thing happened. A massive white owl flew soundlessly across my windscreen, and disappeared into the night. I will swear to this day, that owl looked right at me, as if it knew I was there. At that very same moment, the radio which I had not realised was on, started playing *Take It Easy*… I shivered all the way up and down my spine, and I knew that, once again, my girl had come to give me comfort. (…and thy Comforter shall come…)

# *Pat's Miracle*

Our friend, Pat, whom we had met on our trip to the USA, had a few little miracles of her own, and has often had something happen that she knows is Sandy reaching out and helping her. But one in particular stands out above the rest.

Pat, Bill and Jill were three wonderful characters from London. Sandy and I loved them to bits. We had some great fun and after our holiday, we kept in touch. Pat and her sister, Jill, visited Sandy and me one weekend, for a girly get-together at Sandy's house. We drove the poor neighbours to distraction, but we had fun, and no harm was done. It was a one-off!

Pat, Bill and Jill were shocked to the core when they learned of Sandy's death, and travelled all the way up to Grimsby from London for the funeral, for which I am eternally grateful. So is Sandy.

Before they left, I gave them each a gift and a memento from Sandy. I gave Jill a ring of Sandy's, and Pat a bracelet, which both said they would cherish. These were a couple of the items I had retrieved from the house earlier, and which I have no doubt Sandy wanted them to have. Materially, they were pretty worthless, but in sentimental value they were priceless.

Some months later, Pat phoned me. She was very distressed and had called to tell me she had lost Sandy's bracelet. She was devastated. I had the strongest feeling that she hadn't 'lost' it, just mislaid it. I have a very strong belief in the power of prayer, and I do feel there is much unseen help around when we need it, and if only we can ask for it. Someone once told me that if ever I lost anything, I could ask St Anthony, Finder of Lost Things (and, no doubt, of other things) so I immediately offered up a request, visualising the bracelet as I did. I cannot think why, but at the time, I didn't think to ask Sandy to help, too. I guess it was too close to her passing, and I was still feeling numb and disconnected.

I was absolutely sure the bracelet would turn up somehow, but Pat was willing to believe that it had gone forever, as she believed Sandy had. Pat was employed as a cleaner in a local school and it was here that the bracelet had somehow disappeared. She thought it had somehow come loose and slipped from her wrist, but despite extensive searches, the bracelet was nowhere to be found. The caretaker was informed, and all members of staff and the children were asked to keep their eyes open in case it turned up, but nothing happened.

Some weeks later, I received a phone call from Pat. She could barely get her words out for excitement. The bracelet had been found. She told me that because she was so upset by her carelessness that she had appealed to Sandy for help in finding the bracelet. Simultaneously, I had also decided to ask for Sandy's help. Within days of this request, the school caretaker had been sorting out the wheelie bins in the schoolyard, and as he rolled one away from the wall, there was the bracelet, underneath the wheel of the bin! The delicate bracelet was undamaged, which was a miracle in itself. How it got there is the biggest mystery, as Pat insists that all areas had been searched, including the bin areas.

We concluded happily that our dear Sandy had been instrumental in locating the bracelet, even leading the unsuspecting caretaker to find the treasure. I wonder if he will ever know how much of a miracle he was part of.

## Turkey – she came on holiday with us!

Paul and I had been together for some time before we decided it was time to take a much-needed break. For me, the thought of going anywhere in the world since my trip to America with Sandy had been unthinkable. The idea of 'getting away from it all' and enjoying some sea and sun was very tempting and Paul was sounding me out for a few weeks before surprising me one day. I returned home from work to find him waving two air tickets in front of me.

"We're off to Turkey for a week, is that okay with you?"

"The Hell It Is! When do we fly?"

"Last week in October. It should still be very hot and sunny," grinned Paul, and we set about making our arrangements.

October soon came and the day before our departure we were so excited we couldn't sleep. I was feeling some anxiety because going somewhere on a plane brought painful memories to the surface, but I needed to lay some of my ghosts.

I needn't have worried. Sandy made it quite clear she was with us. After we arrived in Turkey and settled ourselves into the hotel room, we changed and went to find somewhere to have dinner. As we strolled along the beautiful beach, I remarked that the sky resembled a Tequila Sunrise, when suddenly the sound of a familiar tune stopped us in our tracks.

As we sought out the source of the music we couldn't believe our eyes. There, in an Old Wild Western style saloon bar, was a bunch of cowboys line dancing to the tune of *Take it Easy*!

Tears pricked my eyes, but I couldn't be unhappy, because this was one more message from my girl to say she was still here. There were many more signs on this holiday, but Sandy and the Eagles' Welcoming Committee moment is one that one stands out!

# *The Chunnel*

1 March 2002.

After a horrendous night tossing and turning, I finally drifted off. I became aware that I was dreaming. In the dream I was in my office at work, with a friend and work colleague, and one other female unknown to me. Suddenly the phone rang at my desk. I picked it up and as clear as a bell, I could hear Sandy on the other end of the line.

"Hiya, it's me!" she said excitedly. I replied, delighted to hear her voice. Then it dawned on me that this was no ordinary telephone call.

Sandy was so excited to be able to chat to me, and I was aware of the brevity of the call. I remembered that I'd been reading about something called the Violet Flame Decree prior to falling asleep, and I had also read a couple of chapters of Sandy Stevenson's fascinating book, *The Awakener*. I knew, even in the dream, this was a special thing happening. I was experiencing a feeling of electricity tingling all the way up my spine, for the entire time Sandy was talking to me.

Jayne, the lady in the office, then became aware that my caller was not of this world, and her face was a picture! I could hardly speak, but managed to reply to Sandy even though my throat ached with grief.

I found it difficult to speak, as I was crying but Sandy continued to chat, saying that she wanted to contact me. I asked her how in Heaven she had managed to do this, and she said, "Oh, I just decided I wanted to do it, so I'm 'chunnelling' – sort of like channelling, but like a telephone line." (This conversation was conveyed to me telepathically. Sandy explained that when a soul has reached a certain level of awareness, and the vibrations are matching those of the person on Earth, a communication channel – or chunnel! – can be opened up). It is also possible for our technology to be utilised.

This is only one means of communication that our loved ones can use; if we can refine our vibrations enough to cross the bridge… it's a two-way road, so to speak. It made so much sense to keep trying to enlighten my soul, and gave me such an injection of Joy.

I was still overjoyed, and when she told me about the channelling communication, I said to her (laughing excitedly), "Wait 'til I put THIS in the book!"

We laughed together, and I knew it was important for me to wake up and remember this information.

I knew then that our communication was coming to a close, and I said, "Sand, are you still there?" My voice was breaking with emotion, because I was so sad to have to say goodbye again.

She sounded very faint, and I knew our conversation was a treasure I couldn't hold for much longer. The important bit was that I remembered and wrote it down. As our connection faded away, I saw the older lady in the dream gazing upon me with concern…

I woke up crying. My pillow soaked with tears. It was 6.38am. I ran down the stairs to find my journal with *Take It Easy* playing in my mind. I knew my girl had been telling me she was around for me, and what's more, the veils between our worlds were getting thinner.

I blessed Sandy, and asked her to call me later, which she did. But that's another story.

# The Chunnel 2

July 7th, 2003 – Sandy called me on the 'chunnel' again last night. I went to bed and fell into a deep sleep.

I was at work and the phone rang. Picking it up I heard Sandy as clear as a bell saying to me, "Hiya Jewel, it's me again. I've found a better connection and it's a lot clearer now so I can talk for longer."

I was speechless at first, but realised we had to get in as much conversation as we could before the connection faded. We chatted for ages and I asked her about our book. "Sand, what about our book?" (Work of Heart, as it was then).

"Yes, it's definitely going to be out there, don't worry about it," and as she said this, her voice began to crackle and fade.

I felt a mixture of emotions but mostly happiness as I woke up and felt her energy with me in the room.

Not surprisingly, when I switched on the radio one of our songs was playing: *Daydream Believer*!

# Sandy's Message through Judith's Card

In 2002 I began working for the Children's Rights organisation as an administrator. I absolutely loved the job. Apart from making loads of new friends, my work colleagues were working with kids from backgrounds similar to mine, and I felt as if the Universe had found me my dream job!

One of the wonderful young people's advocates who worked occasionally from my office base was called Judith. She and I instantly hit it off and I loved chatting to her whenever she came into the office. She was extremely good at her job and the kids loved her because of her empathy toward them and her wonderful sense of humour.

One weekend, I was home alone because Paul was working again. Getting through the week was okay while I was at work, but weekends sometimes caught up with me, emotionally, and I was feeling really low. I had been dreaming about Sandy again and missing her dreadfully.

I recall sobbing into my morning tea and sitting at the table talking to Sandy in my heart, asking her to be with me. The postman arrived and in the mail was the most unexpected gift – a little Thank You card from Judith to say thanks for sending her some information she needed. I hadn't done anything out of the ordinary, just my job in sending her some stationery and expenses sheets, but that was just like Judith to appreciate every little thing. The beautiful little card showed a picture of a little girl, aged about five, encircled by stars. The caption was: Catch it Quick. It's the stuff dreams are made of!

As I read the card, tears pricked my eyes, because I felt as if Sandy was letting me know she had been in my dream with me. This happened a lot and it took a while for me to realise that she was able to reach me through dreams.

At the time I was reading the card, the radio – once again the medium for Sandy to reach out to me – began playing the Eagles': *New Kid in Town.*

I saw Sandy smile as I felt my heart lift, and I thanked her for once again showing up in a way I couldn't have imagined possible.

## The Sunflower Miracle

The weekend of 31st May 2004 loomed and the familiar feelings of dread and anxiety were plaguing me. I had long since realised that around the time of an anniversary, whether I realised it or not, my body would remember and throw up all kinds of emotions. My friend, Sian, called to invite me to dinner that evening with a friend of hers and I had agreed to go.

Leaving Paul at home, I went into Oswestry town to do the weekly shopping. Having done that, I mooched around the town centre intending to visit the market. I noticed a market stall on the corner of the street and as I looked over to their display, the sight of giant sunflowers caught my eye. My heart began to pound and I felt dizzy. I had not seen sunflowers so beautiful for some time, and definitely not for sale on a flower stand. Immediately, Sandy was by my side. My mind filled with pictures of her funeral and the giant sunflowers I had taken to the service with me.

I stood transfixed for about five minutes, with my emotions doing somersaults inside, and then I could stand it no longer. I began to feel tears welling up and I wanted to run, run, run... Somehow I ended up at the car park, wrenched the car door open, and sank into the seat sobbing. I managed to drive myself home, but it was as if a hole had opened up in my soul again, and I was inconsolable. Paul was brilliant with me, and I asked him to ring Sian and cancel my evening. There was no way I could go out feeling like I did. I would be dreadful company.

Sian was really wonderful. She was always very understanding but also very practical and down to earth.

"I know it hurts, but I think you need to come out with us," she coaxed. I couldn't speak for crying, and she continued to talk to me, and said that if I really didn't want to come that was okay, but gave me some time to think about it.

I put the phone down feeling completely wretched. Just then, I heard the strains of *Daydream Believer* from the garden. Paul and I looked at one another in disbelief. The radio, which had not been switched on, burst into life and The Monkees brought me back to my senses.

"It's Sandy, darling," said Paul, gently.

"I think you're right," I agreed. "I will go out tonight. It will do me good. She wouldn't want me to sit home being miserable, I know that now."

Fast forward to the evening and I drove to Sian's trying to feel cheerful. We drove to Sian's friend's farmhouse to pick up Kate, then intended going on to a local country hostelry for food. As I walked up the path to Kate's house, the first thing that greeted me was a giant sunflower growing in a pot outside the front door. My spine tingled, and Sian looked at me as she had noticed it too. As I walked into Kate's lovely farmhouse kitchen, she greeted me with a warm hug that was full of love. She reminded me of Sandy. As she went to fetch my drink, my eyes fell upon the most beautiful vase – decorated with A SUNFLOWER!

When we arrived at the pub we found they had stopped serving food so we had to get back in the car and find an alternative.

We found a lovely old place not far from the first one, and as we pulled into the car park, we all noticed that outside the front of the pub were huge tubs of sunflowers!

Once inside, I went to the bar to order some food and a young man sitting at the bar on a tall bar stool turned to me and for no reason at all greeted me with, "Aloha!" (Mine and Sandy's greeting to one another ever since we had been on Waikiki Beach in Oahu, Hawaii). Oh! And he just happened to be wearing a T-shirt with OAHU, HAWAII emblazoned across the front.

I couldn't contain my joy. All of these things were signs from Sandy. I knew it without a shadow of doubt. They were all significant things between us and you couldn't have written this script if you'd tried.

I had a very lovely evening and by the end of it I felt very much better. On the way home, I looked up to the heavens and said to Sandy, "Thank you my wonderful Sunflower Angel, for getting me through this day," and as a final goodnight, the most brilliant shooting star blazed a trail of silver light across the sky.

No doubt about her presence. None whatsoever.

## The Guardian Angel

As I was looking out of the window, overcome by another bout of sobbing after attempting to write more memories of my lovely girl, I sent a wish out to the Universe. I talked to Sandy in my heart and asked her to wait for me and to promise me that as soon as I returned home to where she was, she would come and meet me. I want her to be the first person I see. Suddenly, I heard a tinkle from the top corner of the room. Sitting on my bookcase was a beautiful little guardian angel doll that my beautiful Aunty Myra had sent to me one day, as a surprise gift. This little angel has a key in her back and when you wind her up, she dances, waves her little wand and her head moves from side to side to the tune of *Ave Maria*. The angel had been sitting on top of the bookcase for the best part of three years, unwound and silent. In answer to my silent prayer, this little angel suddenly moved and tinkled, only once. She fell silent and has not been wound since nor has she made a move or a sound.

Once again, I knew that my very own guardian angel, Sandy had answered my prayer.

## The Telephone Call from Heaven

This story is still as fresh in my mind as the day it happened. It was Saturday, 13th July 2002 and I was having one of my 'missing her' days and had gone to sit in the garden with the radio and my thoughts. I was deeply unhappy and trying not to be. This is exactly how I wrote the account of the day in my journal:

Saturday 13th July 2002 (weird energy weekend)…

Something really weird just happened. Paul got up from his night shift. I was in the garden. I went inside to make tea, while he settled in the deckchair to catch the sunshine. Returning with the tea, we started chatting about my day so far, as Paul could see I wasn't myself. I began to sob uncontrollably, talking about Sandy and how much and how deeply I missed her and how deep the pain went. I told him I didn't think I could possibly open my heart again as it hurt too much to feel.

A few minutes later, we heard the phone ring. It only rang twice and then stopped. Paul went inside to see who had called. He didn't come out immediately so I went to find out who the call had been from.

Paul was sitting in his chair looking very pale.

"Are you okay?" I asked, tentatively.

"I dunno really. Something really weird just happened," answered a very perturbed Paul.

He asked me to pick up the phone to see if we had a dial tone, which I did, and we had. "Then something strange is going on," he said, and he dialled 1471 to find out the number of the caller. He listened and then repeated the number to me, which was a mobile number.

"But that's your mobile phone number," I gasped. Paul didn't believe me, saying that was impossible. He could never remember the number of his own phone anyway and went to double check. His mobile was in his workbag, zipped up and locked away. The number was his!

Paul then told me that he'd picked up the house phone to answer it, and all he could hear was breathing, like the laboured breathing of someone in difficulty. He put the phone down and then picked it up again, to see if the line had cleared and it hadn't, in fact there was nobody there, but also there was no dial tone. That is why he asked me to check the dial tone when I came into the house to see if the line was working. Which, by the time I came in, it was.

The time of the call on the house phone was 14:30. The time of the last call made from the mobile phone – *to our house phone* – was 14:43. Which meant that his phone had called our house phone all by itself (!) at 14 minutes *AFTER* the call to the house. None of it made sense. Except that we both stood there, chills running up and down our spines feeling Sandy's presence all around us. "It's Sandy, isn't it?" grinned Paul. "There is no other explanation."

At that precise moment, *Alternate Title* by The Monkees, burst into life on the radio in the garden....Make no mistake, Love will always find a way.

Sunday 14th (the following day):

Paul was standing by the washing machine, when he felt a sudden gentle touch on his head and shoulder. Turning round expecting me to be standing behind him, there was nobody there. At that moment, *All things bright and beautiful* came on the radio. That was Uncle Ted's favourite hymn and was played at his funeral. It seemed that Sandy was definitely trying to get our attention that weekend.

## *Extracts from The Virtual Memorial Garden*

I found this wonderful life-saving website purely by accident, if there is such a thing. After Sandy was cremated, her sister took away her ashes and that was that. I know that being Sandy's sister she had the right, and must have also felt she needed to have something of her sister close to her, but that simple act broke my heart. I had nowhere to take my grief and pain. There was no grave to visit and no memorial where I could lay flowers occasionally. I do think these things are important in the grieving process, as they help you to come to terms with the separation and loss.

The VMG is a website created for people like me, who need to have their grief validated. You can create an obituary to your loved one and you can then visit your special page and add bits to it, whenever you feel the need. It saved my sanity and I will be eternally grateful for that.

To be able to put something down to honour Sandy's memory was incredibly healing for me. I shed oceans of tears during the process, but always came away feeling cleansed and refreshed. The obituary isn't exclusive to the person who created it, either. Other people can also visit and put their thoughts and feelings down, too. I have extracted some of my ramblings here, so you get the idea of the process. These were my authentic feelings at the time of writing.

### Sandra (Sandy) Coulbeck

#### 31 May 1956 - 16 Jul 1997

*Gone but not forgotten, you were a light in my life that has gone out, and it temporarily left me in the dark. But I'm ok now, and though I will always miss you, my darling cousin, I will never forget you.... see you later, all my love for all time, Julie... xxxxx*

This was the very first message I wrote after I discovered the site. Looking at the words now, I can see so clearly that my journey had only just begun. I was completely unaware of how deep my grief went, but at this stage, it was enough to be able to say something. I needed to place Sandy on a page somewhere, even if it was in cyberspace, so I could see and touch something of her memory. I didn't have a gravestone so this became my touchstone. We all need touchstones in our lives. Much later, I found the courage to express my feelings more deeply. The following is extracted from the diary of that journey.

*28 Apr 1999*

Dearest Sandy, it is almost two years since you went away, and the pain is beginning to ease just a little. When I wrote the first memorial, the pain still felt like a gaping hole in my heart, and my head could not cope with finding words my heart could not say. However, since you went away, you have given me more proof than I could ever need of your continued existence. I don't know where your beautiful energy resides. It doesn't matter where it is. All that matters is that I KNOW you are with me. I know that when I really need a helping hand, you are right there to give me strength and courage to go on. I have found it so very hard not having you around. You were not just my cousin, because having been born only six weeks apart (me the older one, of course) you were my soul mate. You were my sister, my partner in crime, my laughter and my tears... The hardest thing about all of this is no-one could ever replace you. Nobody could ever have the same sense of humour as you. Nobody could ever make me laugh 'til I wanted to burst, like you could. Nobody has been there for me, heart, soul, mind, loving cuddles and every other way you supported and loved me... I don't know when the pain will stop, if ever, although, as I said, it gets easier to deal with. Sometimes I'll hear one of 'our songs', or see the Grand Canyon on the TV. The other day, I saw your beloved San Francisco on a travel programme, and it is these things that make me break apart once again... just when I think I've gotten over you! I know that you come to me in my dreams, and I know you visit me sometimes in the dark of the night when my soul is crying for comfort. I also know you won't carry me... or do it for me... that is my job. But knowing I haven't really lost you for good helps. Knowing somewhere deep in my heart and soul, the bits that go beyond all logic, I will see you again someday. I know you've only moved into 'another room' - sometimes I hear you, but I can't see you. Geoff and Sheila miss you. I know they do. I don't see them much. After your house was sold, I couldn't bear to go down the avenue again. Or visit them. But Geoff sent me a beautiful calendar the first Christmas after you went away... it was a Christian Lassen calendar. I couldn't believe it. I still have your beautiful Lassen print which you bought in Hawaii on our trip, Summer of '96... it is in pride of place in the house and everyone who sees it loves it. Pat rang me the other night. She misses you too... she says that to have known you for just a short while after making a friend for life on our American trip, and then to lose you, is painful for her, so God knows what it must be like for me. I know God knows how I feel. I know you do. I gotta go now. Aloha and Maholo my darling ... I love you and always will... 'til we meet again... Jewel xxx

*14 Jul 1999*

My Darling Sand. It is Wednesday, 14th July 1999 and two years ago, you passed from this life. The pain is still there inside but I want you to be happy wherever you are until we meet up again. I am sure that we will know another life and existence together at some point in time, but some days, I wish with all my heart I could be evolved enough to SEE you... to part the veil that I am sure separates us... I can feel you; I know you are still with me when I need you. I hear our songs – in fact, I heard *San Francisco* by Scott McKenzie only today, as I was sending you my love. I really know this is your way of telling me you're still around. If you can, darling girl, help me to be brave and strong. Help me to grieve but not to hang on, help me to let go of you but never forget you... I want you to be happy, really I do. I love you with all my heart, Sand... there could never be another you.... 'til we meet again.... all my heart and soul, your Jewel.... xxx

*19 Nov 1999*

Hiya Sand…it's me! Just checking in again. I tried to write the other night, but it didn't accept my message for some reason. I was just going to tell you that it was Remembrance Day. I know you loved to remember your Dad on that day, and were so proud to have his war medals adorning your hallway walls... Bless you darling. Anyway, I saw four rainbows on the way to work today. Did you send them? I thought maybe you did because as I looked at them, two songs came into my mind at the same time… *Desperado*, by the Eagles, and *Rainbow*, by Marmalade. They were two of our many special songs and I always feel you close to me when I hear them. The sky was beautiful. It was just so different everywhere I looked… do you remember when we used to go out in the car with your dad and when it was raining on the horizon, he would say, "Look kids, rain on the horizon…" and he'd tell us which way it was falling. I thought he was magic and it was all a miracle. I miss you very much today. I haven't been too happy lately, again. I thought, on the way to work today, that I seem to have lost my kindness button… I thought of your infinite kindness and how you always had it in plentiful supply when somebody needed it. Especially me. You were so much better at kindness than me. Please will you help me to see how I can get mine back and make it grow? I know if you were here you would help me, however you could. Winter is coming…and with it, the cold. Cold always feels so unloving and unrelenting, but then sometimes we need cold, because the frost gets rid of bugs and nasties, doesn't it? I think I am going to have a Christmas tree this year, and put some lovely old baubles on it (if I can find some) and an angel on the top. I shall call the angel Sandy! That will be something, won't it? Me, having a Christmas tree. You know how I feel about Christmas! I know how much you loved it when you were here, and I shall revive your spirit of love in this little gesture. I can't bear to do anything too big, my heart still hurts a lot when things remind me of our time together, but I guess a little tiny tree and maybe even a small stocking at the end of Paul's bed might help me to get my kindness muscle going again. It is very stuck… sometimes I think I need a major miracle to open up my heart again. It seems so hard to do, Sand. I wish you were here to hug me. Selfishly, I wish that. But kindness, like everything else, is like a muscle that needs daily exercise, isn't it? If we go to the gym, or take a long walk when we've been sitting around doing nothing, it hurts the first time… the second time gets a little easier and in time, you feel a whole lot better for exercising. I love you with all my heart, and I miss you terribly. I pray that when it's my turn to come home, you'll be there to greet me and I hope we can plan more time together in future lifetimes wherever they may be… Yours, always 'Jewel' xxxxxxxxxxxxx

*9th January 2000*

Hi again, Sand… well, we've just had Christmas, as you know, and it was brilliant. I hope you liked the little tree I put up for you… It was the only way I could do it, by doing it for you. Did you like the angel Paul bought for me? We called it Sandy, after you, and she shone from the top of the tree for the whole of the holiday. Something happened this Christmas. I think I have turned a corner, for real. My heart feels much better, like it's been packed in ice for so long, and it's beginning to thaw out and get well again. It is taking a bit of exercising to get it sorted out, but it's only like exercising a muscle that's atrophied, bound to be a bit painful at first! I am planning to write a book about you. Well, about you and me, really, and about how nobody really dies, not really. I think maybe that is what you and me came to do, you know. I always thought we'd be in this life together forever, 'til we both 'died', but maybe God had other plans? We can still work together, it's just taking time to adjust to how different vibrations prevent us doing things we could have done without much effort here on Earth... Anyway, girl, I would like your help with the book. I can write stuff down, but I want the book to be an inspiration and a help to all those people who are grieving, to let them know that nobody goes away from them, they just change form. I want this book to reach thousands of hearts, and I want it to help them heal, as I have done. Also, to know that there is a way to bridge the gap between your world and ours... So I need all the memories I can remember. You know stuff I have forgotten, so if you could give me a gentle nudge, now and again, I'd be grateful. Well sweetie, it's Sunday and a lovely sunny day. I'm going for a quick walk later - you can join me if you like... I love you more than ever before, and I'll see you later... all my love, your 'Jewel' xxxxx

*06 Mar 2000*

Hi Sand... just a little note to tell you I love you very much and to ask for your help. Paul got made redundant today from his job. He's been there about 17 years so as you can imagine, it was a bit of a blow to him. He's scared, Sand. Can you send him some of your special love and healing, and maybe a Job Fairy or two? *smile* I'm not too worried, but I know he is, and he's trying to be brave for me and himself. I want to help him all I can and I know you can help by sending your special energy. Love you lots sweetie... all my love for now, Jewel xxx

*16 Apr 2000*

Hi babe... it's my birthday next week, but then, you already know that! (big grin). I have so much to tell you, but I guess you already know what is going on around me, because I know you are with me all the time. Hey, what about *Mamma Told Me Not To Come* being in the charts again? I had to laugh, as I recalled how, in our teenage years, we'd dance and sing to it, pretending we were Pan's People (Sand's People, I think we called ourselves)! I was telling my friend Sally at work the other day about how you and I would do advertisements for sweets (Parkes Sherbert Lollipops was the favourite) and how we made up our own words to *Bonnie and Clyde* - then did a performance for my dad, who fell about laughing at our antics! God, didn't we have some fun? Well, things are looking up in the Paul's job stakes, thank you for any input (I can't believe you haven't done something!) and hey, did you see Frank Boyd in the paper this morning? I never realised how much like your dad he looks... no wonder you used to think he was marvellous! Did I tell you that Pat Holmes's daughter, Georgia, lives next door to us now? God what a surprise when I realised who she was. Oh, and at Anna's fashion show the other night, I saw Evelyn who used to go out with Dave Barton (he is as bald as a billiard ball, now)! She is still as lovely as ever. It was Granny Lauder's birthday on 14th of April. Mine next week and yours in May. I shan't forget to put flowers in the beautiful vase you bought me. What would you like? You'll have to tell me! BTW, was that you in my dream the other night? I felt you were trying to let me know that things are going to work out and that something good and sweet is coming to me from the past! I hope so. What a nice birthday surprise that would be! Well girl, please send me money for my birthday if you can... I'd rather have you for one day, mind you, but that can't be, just yet. So I'll try and do something that will remind me of our birthdays past together. Maybe play The Monkees and dance around a bit of cake!!! Well, my darling, I'd better go and talk to somebody I can touch... I miss you like crazy sometimes... the pain subsides, but then, still after all this time, I feel a sharp stab in my heart when a special memory surfaces, and I know I'll never be over you, not really. I will just learn to live without you. I just know that I am happy as long as I know I'll be with you again one day... I love you dearly, darling one... all my love for now... Jewel xxx

*31 May 2000*

HEY GIRL! WOOHOO! - HAPPY BIRTHDAY MY BEAUTIFUL SAND!!! It's your turn now... It's a gloriously sunny day, but what else could I expect? The sun always shines on this day, like it always did... I'm playing *Horse With No Name* by America as I write this, because it is our special America song (well, one of them) and it reminds me of America... I just finished writing to someone who asked who 'Sandy' was, because I'd mentioned you to them in an email message, and I can't cry much as I'm at work at the moment... but I want to, so much. You would love email, Sand. I just know you'd have made tons of friends all over the world via this medium, and it would have been a lot cheaper than the phone!!! It's amazing how far things have progressed on the planet since you moved on. We have internet and email and with your computer, you'd have been hooked up most of the day and night, I know you would. I've made contact with Giovanna again. She and Val are not together anymore, but I guess you'll know that already. It is a great comfort to know there's another person who knew you, and more importantly, who shared our America trip. God, Sand, I'll never ever forget that. It is still too painful to even contemplate going there without you. One day, I promise I'll be brave... Oh girl, it doesn't get any easier... today, I miss you so much that there is a big aching lump in my heart, and my throat. I want to go home and just have a good weep, with Paul, cos he understands about you and me. Later on, I'm gonna get you some flowers and a lovely card. I know it doesn't matter to you because you're not here to see them, but I know you CAN see them, and it matters to me. I never had the money to do all that stuff when you were with me, and now I have, and you're not here... Ironic, eh? Which flowers would you like? Tell me, and I'll know. I'm going to go down to our little café, at St Anthony's Bank, and watch the kites fly over our favourite bit of beach. Remember? We walked there, near where the caravan was, and we planned our holiday, just before we went that summer... oh, we were SO excited. Oh, Sand, I haven't got anybody I can talk to like you... nobody in the world. Our talks in the car at night, when we were kids... scaring each other to death talking about stars, universes, planets, ghosts and all the important things in life... oh, and BOYS!!! I bought a sherbet lollipop the other day, and our 'advertisement song' came into my mind... I know you remember it - my dad nearly bust a gut laughing at us... OH AND GUESS WHAT I FOUND AGAIN? Sweet Tobacco!!! I guess you were with us in Lincoln on Saturday when Anna and I found the sweet shop, but as you know, I've been searching for it forever... and I was just SO happy because it's not about the sweets, it's about the childhood memory. You have to help me save our café, Sand. The council want to shut it and put up a Parking Lot... Sod that! I'm up in arms, and I could use your 'Red Mist' energy, if you can, please?

Anyway, I'm going to have a Margarita, too. I found a recipe for the one we had at the hotel at LAX Airport on our final day in San Francisco, before we came home. Oh, God, wasn't that awful? I hated going home, but I know you were looking forward to it, because that was where your heart was. But for me, it was different. I have a home, now, Sand. I know you'll know this already, but Paul has given me so much in sharing his home with me, and helping me to calm down and stop whizzing off like a demented butterfly... I was searching for so long. I envied you so much having your mum and dad, and a lovely stable home life. But, hey, I've got it now, so that's okay, isn't it? Well sweetheart, I will sign off for now. Just wanted to send you all my love and wish you a Happy Birthday in Heaven... Bye for now, Angel... I miss you... Your Jewel xxxxxx

*11 Jun 2000*

Sand... just a quick pop in to say 'hi!' and tell you I spoke to 'P' the other evening (the day after your birthday, actually). She sends you her love... as you know, she is having major problems with money. I know you'd have helped her if you could, but I guess with some people it is impossible. Anyway, I was talking about you yesterday, to Jill, mum's lodger, and I just lost it again... sorry, girl. I've been having strange dreams about you and Uncle Ted and Aunt Joyce. Say hello to them for me, won't you? I feel you all near me at the moment. Ask Uncle Ted to help Paul with his job, will you? And thank him for helping me with my car... I just felt he had a hand in it somewhere, getting it through its MOT!!! I do believe in miracles. Remember the time you found all those new spindles in your attic for the banister? We thought your dad had made them, especially since you had heard banging and scraping about up there, some weeks prior to that... tee hee! Well sweetie, I just finished watching 'our desert' on telly. The buffalos and the Sonora Desert and Arizona. When I go again, and I WILL, I know you'll come with me, and I'm off now to make a Margarita and to drink your health! I LOVE YOU... 'til later, Jewel xxx

*26 Jul 2000*

Just a quick one darling... passing through to read up on your messages, just to comfort me and bring you closer... Heard *Peaceful Easy Feeling* the other day on the radio. I'm sorry - I know you understand how deep the pain goes. Can't help the crying still, but I wouldn't want it to distress you. Never mind. I felt your arms around me. Anyway, I forgot to tell you about another of my 'Sandy Miracles' as they've come to be known... the other night (16th July, would you believe!!! Happy Deathday!!!) I just happened to switch on the telly to a channel I didn't know was there. There was a movie on called *The Wings of Eagles* and it was a John Wayne movie!! (scream)!! It was all about Pearl Harbour, and can you believe this? Kwajalein was on there, too... remember in Arizona where we saw John Bird's name? That was on as well. I spoke to my friend, Pat, in the US about it, and he said he's a John Wayne fan and also visited the SS Arizona!!! WOW! That's not all... Following the movie was this advertisement for an internet company called... sandy@onthebeach.com HOW AMAZING IS THAT? Oh Sand, I just know with all my heart and soul, every day, that you have really not gone anywhere. I was watching this other thing on the TV and there was this man who had 'died' and he was trying to tell his loved one on Earth that he hadn't gone anywhere. Like Paul always tells me, and I know you use him to communicate with me sometimes, you are only as far away as a feeling or a thought. I love you more now than ever before... one day, I'm going to turn these musings into a book. I think you and I can still work together, Sand... to let people know that there's only a veil between life and death. Another thought occurred to me the other day. As I was thinking about you, and having a weep in the car, I realised why it was that you couldn't feel or see or hear your dad when he passed... it was because you were just too shrouded in grief. Now I know how you felt. At least, some of it, anyway. Well sweetie, I'm going out with Anna tonight.

To a Body Shop thing. It is what your mum would call 'clarts and cack night'!!! tee hee... I love you. With all my heart and soul... 'til we are together again.. and you'd better be there to greet me!!! All yours, Jewel xxxxxxxxxxxxxxxxxxx

*03 Mar 2001*

Oh Sand... gran died yesterday, 2nd March, 8 days before Mum's birthday. I can't begin to describe the pain I feel, but I know that you know. Please, please let me know if you were there to meet her when she came home... it just brought up all the pain of losing you again, only this time it seemed worse, because there are 92 years of remembering in my heart... She came to me and said 'goodbye' and although I didn't get my 'Train Dream' I knew she'd gone... my heart feels like it's breaking, girl. Please hug me and tell Gran I love her... I love you. Your Jewel xxx

*16 May 2001*

Hello precious one... It's been ages since I needed to come here and talk to you, but I know you know I'm always thinking of you... How can I survive without knowing my other half is around me? I suppose you were around tonight when I cried into my dinner and Paul had to give me a huge hug? I wish I could see you, at times like this... I still miss you terribly, and at this time, near your birthday, and death day, the pain comes back into my heart and the 'ice' gets me... I love you... I always will - 'til we meet again... your Jewel xxx

*31 May 2001*

My darling girl... today is your birthday... You would have been 45 yrs old - but I beat you by 6 wks!!! Ha ha... I hope you like the card I got you. It would have been more and I'd have gotten you flowers too, but you know you are in my heart and soul, always. I miss you more than words can ever say. Today, it's bitter sweet painful and lovely all at the same time. They say time heals, Sand, but it ain't goin' away for me. My heart still hurts dreadfully and I still feel like you're going to walk in the door or phone me and make me laugh again. I know you would like Paul. He makes me laugh so much and if you let me know, through him, that you're around me today, I'd be very happy. Say hi to your mum and dad for me. I hope your sister is okay. I don't ever see or hear of her, but I'm sure you are keeping an eye on her and the kids. Our 'Fluff' (my sister) is going through a hard time of it. She has just got her degree and I am really proud of her. I am going to the graduation ceremony. Oh Sand! I wish you would come with me. She's worked so hard at this. I will go and represent her family for her, like you did when Fred from the States came to visit us! hee hee... Well babe... send me a dream or two, eh? And one day, I'll be with you again and we'll visit Hawaii together and take a look at Diamond Head once more... until then, know that I love you with all my heart and soul... God Bless, darling... HAPPY BIRTHDAY... Your Jewel xxxxxxxxxxxxxxxxxxx

*16 Jun 2001*

Oh SAND! Last night was the most awesome night ever, wasn't it? Oh my dear, darling girl, I felt you so strongly by my side at the concert. Did you enjoy it? What a 'stoopid' question eh? I couldn't believe it when my birthday surprise from you and Paul turned out to be 2 tickets to see THE EAGLES in Birmingham!!!!! Oh, God I am so blessed... I love you so much. Thank you for helping Paul to help me... I can't remember my dream about you last night, yet, but I will, I'm sure... I'll be back later, but I have to go meet our Gina now for a shopping trip! I love you... see you later... your 'Jaywol'! xxxxxxxxxx

*13 Aug 2001*

Sand... OMG! I just heard it - *Take It Easy*... was that you? It felt like a message from you. I went outside of the office, as I thought I heard the song, and there was this lady in a big, gold 4-wheel drive car with our song blasting away... not for long, but long enough to make me smile and feel all shivery, and know that you were trying to give me a hug. Oh, Sand... I need you so much right now. I wish I knew what to do. I am trying to pick myself up and feel good but it's just very hard again at the moment. I wish you were here... I really wish that... just for once, to see your face and hold your hand again... oh God, one day, we'll be together again... I know it. Sand, I am really fed up with work. I just don't know what to do about it, and I think I want to leave, but I must replace it with something that my heart and soul is in... but what? Can you help me? I feel lost again... I love you... and I'll talk to you again soon. All my love always, Jewel xxxxxxx

*16 Dec 2001*

Oh Sand... how can I put down in words what I have to say? You are all around me. Paul can even feel your presence... Your Christmas Presence... you ARE the gift... Paul keeps hearing Greg Lake's *I Believe in Father Christmas*. That's the one you loved so much and it makes him cry as well as me. Awww, bless you darling... I keep remembering what you told me when Uncle Ted died and you came to see me... and afterward, when we went to America and I said I could never thank you enough. You told me that I didn't need to because this was your way of thanking ME for giving you the most precious thing of all... *time*. I remember that your dad bought you that watch - I can't find it anywhere, Sand - just prior to him departing in my 'train dream'... I wish that platform was like the one in Harry Potter, and I could just depart on it like they did... and like you all did. Anyway, he bought you the watch and told you he was 'buying you time', time to prepare for his departure... I know how dreadful a time that was for you. It seems that it is the unseen that is the most powerful, isn't it? Like time? You know that my friend Yvonne in Louisiana told me that you and I were 'Heavenly Twins'? Well, she also told me that our souls were one, and that just because your body is no longer around, it doesn't mean your soul, or essence, isn't... she said that when a twin dies, the soul of the two merge into one and can continue living out it's experiences in the one body. I feel this is so true. So much of you has become a part of me. And even though you're not here to talk to and share a hug with, I can still access your wonderful wisdom, if I just listen quietly... It's Christmas time again... and the usual dilemma is going on with me. That time I did it for you was brilliant. It was the most meaningful Christmas I ever had. Paul too. It healed a big part of both of us. So thank you sweet girl, for without you not being here, it wouldn't have happened. The following year was an echo of that and didn't quite reach the same parts, but the thoughts were there. This year, I don't want to 'do' Christmas. But it is so hard to find a balance in this material world, as I'm sure you know. I keep feeling guilty and thinking of the things I 'ought' to do... 'should' do... and I'm trying to only do the things I feel to do. That's very important to me, because Feelings carry Intention and Intention is what people feel... a gift given without Intention lacks love, is what I think. So it is with time, energy, effort, and anything else. I'm feeling a bit blocked again today. Maybe it's the 'Curse' hanging around. Or maybe I just feel a bit emotional. Anna is coming over after she's spent Christmas with her dad. I want to make her time here memorable and happy. Making up for lost time, I suppose. It's all about time, isn't it? I went to sleep last night thinking of you. Asking if you could, in some way, let me know what our deal was before we came to this life together. I still find it incredible that I had no inkling of you going away... 40 years together. I anticipated at least another 40... and you went away. I don't, to this day, understand why I didn't know or have prior warning. It still feels like a massive part of me is missing, but maybe I just have to get my head around it a different way and get used to your energy being here in a 'not so material' way? I've been in touch with Paul W. He lived down our street about 6 doors down from us. It is so lovely to talk to someone who knew and remembered you with such kindness and humour. Just to share memories with someone who knew you at all is a healing thing. He remembers you with love and fondness, and that means such a lot to me. His mum is still alive, bless her. He has four lovely kids, an ex-wife, and lives (would you believe) in Australia, near our Sara... isn't that amazing? He remembers Roger N, too (ha ha) and how Roger used to always have a maungy face on him! Miserable bugger! ha ha... I told him you used to have a crush on him, Big Time, and he thought that was highly amusing!!! I have been hearing 'our songs' in abundance this week. I have your picture on my kitchen counter, so I can see your beautiful smiling face when I'm cooking, or singing... OH GOD, I WISH YOU WERE HERE SO I COULD HUG YOU... and give you some of that precious time I didn't realise was so precious. You know, Sand... maybe I just got my answer... Time is the most precious gift you can give anyone, isn't it? It costs nothing, and there is an abundance of it... It's unseen, like electricity, but vital, just the same. You can't wrap it up, or even buy it - not really - but in the end, Time and Presence are what matter. I want to write that book about us. I will need your help at times. One day, I'll get down to it.

I swear it. I might need pictures, but I can't get your sister to answer my letters right now, so it might **have to be** picture-less! Oh well... I have you in my memories and others will just have to imagine your beauty. Thank you for your Christmas Presence, darling Sand... I love you so much. I'll try and be really happy, and I will give that which you gave - Time and Presence. That, I can assure you, will be ENOUGH! Thanks for listening... I just needed to touch base with you and know that you could be reached, if only through the medium of the internet world... God Bless, Night Night, Sleep Tight... I love you with all my heart... Jewel xxxxxxxxxxxxxxxxxxxxxx

*26 Dec 2001*

Hiya girl...just needed to touch base with you, as I am not feeling too good today. It's the day after Christmas Day and as you will know, after having done 'your' Christmas for you, we don't feel the same about it anymore and have decided to go back to Plan 'A' and not do Christmas... Oh, Sand, I know you loved it, but it's all changed so much now. We even had a bloody white Christmas, you know? Today, Boxing Day, it's all deep and crisp and even, and I looked out with a mixture of excitement, and nostalgia, and the realisation that things are never gonna be the same. I dreamed about Gran and Grandad Croft last night... well, just before I woke up. It was a curious dream. He was trying his damndest to coax her into being his wife again, and she was having none of it. I fear Gran was a bit of a hard nut to crack... it makes me wonder if this didn't help Grandad's 'illness'... You know Sand, it was a horrible realisation the day I admitted my grandad was a paedophile. Doesn't that sound dreadful? But that is what he was. If he were alive today, Mum and I could have done something to make him pay. Sometimes I think I have healed from all of that stuff, and other days I know there are still wounds and scar tissue. I want to get on with our book, Sand, but Anna's coming today with Ed. Watch over them, and make sure they get here safely, eh? Please don't go away and please continue to help me remember things will you? I know you know this, but this book is really important, Sand. I have to write this to let people know that when their loved ones die, their energy remains. It's a much bigger picture. I panicked the other day as I thought I'd got 'Writers Block'... ha ha - can you imagine that? Writers block, me?

I've only just begun, and it's going to take *time*... As all things do here on Earth. Where you are, I suppose time is a strange energy as it doesn't exist as we know it down here. I am realising a lot of things, and in allowing myself to remember this book, it is helping me to open my heart and mind to other things. But I'll share this with you later. Right now it's only important that I talk to you as I'm having a 'missing you' day again. I tell you what girl, wherever we end up next, we're going to make damn sure they don't do death like they do on Earth... I can't stand all this space, apartness, separation stuff!!! There HAS to be a better way! Well babe, I have to go now, as I've got 'typing shoulders' and I know you know all about that! I'm glad you're not here to do me a massage... you were rubbish at it!!! hee hee.... I love you, I love you, I love you... your Jewel xxxxxxxxxxxxxxxxxxx

*Sunday, 13 Jan 2002*

12:15pm: Oh Sand... thank you, darling. God Bless you for that... it's only just occurred... another Miracle by you... I'm speechless... you came through AGAIN! This time your miracle was shared with Anna. I rang her to talk, as I was missing her. We haven't seen each other or spoken since she and Ed were here at Christmas time, as you know. I do miss her, Sand. Anyway, we chatted about nothing for a while, then got to the nitty gritty. She said she'd been on a low ebb for a few days, and we talked about that for a bit and then I felt to let her know that I've also been very depressed for a couple of weeks. I have been in that place where nobody should have to go, not ever. Dark, terrifying, lonely, and to the point where I even lost you. I couldn't see any light anywhere. In the end, I went to see a lovely lady who is a healer and a counsellor. I know you know all about that, because you were there with me. She confirmed that to me. At the end of my healing session, which made me feel so much better and able to cope again, you came to me and hugged me. I clearly felt and saw your laughing face and we shared a private joke, which made me laugh inside. You told me to 'lighten up' and you were still here with me. The lady who helped me, told me after we'd finished the session that she had felt your presence, which confirmed what I already knew. But it's so much more of a miracle, if that is possible, when someone else confirms it too! That night, I dreamed about you and Uncle Ted and Aunt Joyce for the first time in quite a while. You know how much better that made me feel, I know you do. It confirms for me that you are with them. Your mum looked radiant. Her hair had grown, and she looked plump and happy. I felt a lot of love from her. In the dream, I was in your old house again, but each time I go there, it appears a little different from the last time. It gets 'lighter'. I knew that I had a limited time with you all, and Uncle Ted appeared to me in his old dungarees and that old gnarled up Aran sweater he used to favour! I am not sure if you knitted it for him. He picked me up and swung me around, hugging me, and shouting out to you, "Look who's here, Sand!" As ever, we had a giggle, and I was happy/sad, knowing I couldn't stay and you couldn't come with me either… I sat down on the chair and started to cry. You put your head on my knee and cried with me, but we both knew I had to go. The feeling I had when I woke up was a good feeling. I felt I had broken through a barrier, and I felt that the veil had gotten a little bit thinner, once again. I know I am right, Sand. I feel that if I can keep going forward and finding ever more healing and light for myself, the closer to you I get. One day, I swear, I'm going to prove to people there truly is NO death!

Anyway, I was telling Anna this on the phone, and reassuring her that I understood and empathised with what she might be going through. I encouraged her to know there is always hope and that there is always a light at the end of the tunnel, even though it might be the darkest it's ever been. She said she knew that, and I said that I was trying to write some more of this book but I'd been 'blocked' by my own depression and negativity, and she said the same had happened to her with her art and other stuff. I told her that there was healing available, if she ever needed it, and that you had confirmed to me that you hadn't gone anywhere… and at the exact same moment I said that…. *TAKE IT EASY* CAME ON THE RADIO!!! OH SAND!!! The joy, the elation, the tears… Anna nearly passed out with shock and disbelief… So together my darling girl, we have to carry on this work we set out to do. Even if it's not how I envisaged us doing it! We're still a great team, Sand… Oh, my heart feels so big. Don't leave me, will you? Not ever… your ever loving crazy woman, Jewel xxxxxxxxxxxxxxxxxxx

…some time later…

*Wednesday, 10th March 2010*

Oh Sand. What can I say? Tonight I finally met one of our beloved Monkees, but I know you know that already, because you were there with us. When I heard on Radio Two that Micky Dolenz was appearing in *Hairspray* in London I knew I had to write to him. And yes, I know you prompted me because they played two of our favourite Monkee songs after his interview! Haha… I couldn't have been more surprised when I received a gorgeous signed photo of him a week later and a letter from his beautiful wife, Donna. Can you believe it? Her sister is called Sandy!!! Coincidence or what?

Anna and I travelled to London on the train and we could barely contain our excitement because Micky and Donna wanted to see us after the show, which was fantastic. Micky sounds as good as ever. We went to dinner with them – they are so lovely. We, of course, toasted you with champagne. Only the best for my girl. Of course, I had to take you with me and I showed them your picture, the one of you posing beside the cop car in L.A. So, my darling girl, you got to meet your Monkee after all. Oh, how happy I am… I love you so much. Night night darling!

*Monday 31st May 2010*

Well, I did it! Finally, our Work of Heart is written and recorded – your birthday present this year. I hope I've done us justice. I've just sent it to the lovely publisher, Beth. She is an absolute godsend, bless her. She says our book will be launched in August. And as you know, 1st August is very significant to us both because that is the day we flew to America all those years ago. It's been nearly 13 years since you left me and writing this has been the toughest task I've taken up so far. The last few months have been the hardest as I've had to revisit a lot of painful memories and emotions but I feel at peace now, knowing you've been with me all along, helping me. I am so proud of us. Nobody will be prouder when our words are finally in print. I hope you are proud of me, too, my darling. I know I could have gone on writing forever, partly to keep you with me in a way that makes me feel your presence most strongly, but mainly because it validates who you were, still are and always will be. Happy Birthday my darling... until I see you in Heaven.

# Part 3

# *A Work in Progress*

There are a million and one incidences of Sandy's continued expansion and omnipresence and if I wrote them all down I would be here forever. She continues to visit with me in dreams and to pop by with one of our songs or other wonderful memories and I hope by now you will have a good idea of what our friendship was – and still is - about. I know these accounts of how I dealt with her death may not be grammatically perfect, but they are my feelings at the time of writing. In the name of authenticity, I don't want to change that.

However, it is now 2010 and I've been experiencing more changes and expansions, which have unveiled a whole new dimension to my Life Experience. But that is a whole other book!

The work with Sandy continues and that is why this lifetime experience for every one of us is a Work in Progress. I believe that you can never get it done and you can't get it wrong. If there is one thing that Sandy's 'death' has given me: it is Time. I have cried many tears and my heart has ached and broken many times since she and I parted company, and writing about her has sometimes given me a major headache! But I know that we have a lifetime to experience everything we need to experience and after that is over, we have eternity. In this life, we rush around in our busy lives trying to get things done 'on time'. We set ourselves deadlines for this and that and the other and become stressed and unhappy when we fail to meet our own unrelenting time limits and exacting standards. But that can change. Sandy has helped me to view things from a less restrictive perspective.

Ever since that classroom incident where Sandy and I wrote the same essay, I have always known I wanted to write. I knew I wanted to write things that would touch people's hearts but although I knew I wanted to do this, I didn't have a clue how to begin. Sandy gave me that beginning. I might have chosen a better alternative to having her leave me physically, but there you have it and here we are!

When I was a very small child I experienced something inexplicably wonderful that I never forgot. I can recall to this day in

145

vivid detail how it made me feel. I was lying in my granny's feather bed, aged about two, and I remember a feeling of bliss washing over me as I gazed out at the stars. I used to ask Granny to leave the curtains open so I could look at the moon and stars and hear the pussy cats 'courting' on the tin roof of the factory behind our house! I adored the stars and always felt I belonged there with them, not on the ground. I began to gently expand out of my body, out of the bed, out of the room and out of the house. I wasn't flying. I didn't feel I was simply lifting out of my body. It was a definite feeling of expansion. I was amused at feeling so BIG! I don't recall being one bit afraid, simply fascinated. I continued to expand out into the Universe and beyond the stars, and it seemed that the Universe was expanding into me at the same time. I know I felt as if I was part of everything and it was part of me and the retaining memory I have is of knowing that I was not just a flesh, bone and blood body. As I began to return to my body, contracting now, the most wonderful benevolent and loving energy spoke to me. It wasn't an audible voice; it was more the feeling of energy being translated by me into words. Of course at that age one doesn't have verbal skills but more importantly, one has emotional memory. At least I did. I remember that the feeling was of the most all-encompassing love I had ever felt.

The voice told me that this is who I really was. It said that I had come to experience Life on Earth and that one day, I would know what I had specifically come to do. I was told I had a special job to do on Earth and that I was loved and protected. The beautiful voice faded… and in the morning, I didn't remember a thing.

Having, therefore, always been aware of my inner being or soul as some would refer to it, I know that a part of me lives where Sandy now resides. I know this place as the Source. It is where she, as a vibrant energy being, continues.

Throughout my earlier years I found myself shying away from religion and spirituality, because my mother spent her life running from one fortune teller to another in an effort to find comfort. She was a very unhappy lady, but didn't realise she had the power to make positive changes in her life. I could see what she needed to do, but in many ways Mum was emotionally very unstable and what you would call 'weak minded'. Although try telling that to my Dad! She could be incredibly opinionated on one subject or another, but when it came to emotional intelligence she flunked her exams! Bless her...

I know that as a child I was fascinated by and very curious about many things and always asked a lot of questions, much to the chagrin of my mother and granny. Each would say to me when confronted with yet another off-the-wall query, "Go ask your gran," or, "Go ask your mother," and neither of them knew the answers to my endless supply of questions. It was many years before I found the answers I'd been seeking, and I discovered along the way that there are 'many who are called but few are chosen'. What this means, to me, is that although many people want to be psychic, or clairvoyant or to be mediums or healers, they want this so desperately that they sacrifice their integrity and authenticity for the glory. Not all the people I encountered were like this, but many were. I don't think they are bad people, nor do I think they are wrong to do what they do. They are simply on a journey, as are we all.

I believe we are all capable of extraordinary things. I believe that if you are being true to yourself and are maintaining a healthy balance in your life, all that you desire will come to you. If you are a natural medium, you will know it. You will want to do it and it will bring you joy. And others.

My encounters with charlatans provided wonderful contrast for me. Without them doing something I did not want to do, I could not have had a basis for comparison for my own process when it came along. For a long time, my low self-esteem gave such people dominion over me. I didn't think I could possibly be as aware as most of these people. After all, they were practising their craft and making money at it. Years later I discovered I had been more advanced in my knowing than any of them!

The voices were true to their word. All my life, despite living through some precarious experiences and following many false premises, I have felt somehow protected. I can see looking back over the course of my life that my awakening, or expansion, has occurred organically and naturally. The expansion I experienced as a two-year old has taken place physically and is continuing to do so. The energy of the Source from whence we came is always with us. It is who we are. There is no separation, which was also part of my expansion experience.

Our loved ones don't leave us. Sandy's friendship was the deepest human relationship I have ever known bar none. Nothing can hurt me like losing her, so I feel protected by that unique love and I am eternally grateful for her presence in my life.

Sandy feels as though she is a part of me, even more so now. The way I have come to know this is through my own experience and acceptance of what feels right and good to me. I have a premise nowadays and that is, 'If it feels good, do it. If it doesn't – don't!'

Thus, Sandy continues to chat with me every day in some way or another and frequently when I'm travelling in the car alone, she will pop in and sit by me. As soon as I feel her energy, I start giggling. She always brings Joy. Never Sadness. Not anymore.

I am now more aware of myself than ever before and with Sandy's help and cooperation I know this wonderful life experience will continue to expand into more and more fun. The other day I was sitting in my garden, writing, when I stopped for a moment. I was stuck for words for a change!

I was suddenly aware of my beautiful girl standing in front of me, proffering something in her hand. It felt as though she had reached into my heart and in doing so, she whispered, "Solomon has always been with you, my Jewel. Throughout your life, he has been with you, don't you see?" and she held out her hand to reveal a tiny little owl brooch. The brooch was the very first birthday gift I ever bought for her when we were only eight years old…

Kim and I had fun today, positioning the pool in the garden, ready for summer. It is a hot, beautiful, blue-sky day. We have the music centre with us and as I cool off in the pool I am moved to change the music. I twiddled the iPod and found the beautiful song, *Over the Rainbow* by the late, great Israel Kamakawiwo'ole. He was a giant of a man, physically and spiritually, as was Sandy (albeit she was a girl!) I lost myself in the beautiful music with the Aloha Hawaii tune and I swayed in Hula dancing style to the hypnotic song in the cool water, imagining for a moment I was back in the South Pacific, watching Diamond Head across the sparkling ocean.

When I returned to Planet Earth, Kim asked me who was singing that lovely song, and I told him. As I had access to the internet, I looked up Israel's details. I felt the familiar tingles up the spine as I realised that not only had Israel lived and died on Oahu (Sandy's and my favourite Hawaiian island) but he was born as a Gemini (as was Sandy) and he passed in June 1997, a month before Sandy.

I don't know why I shivered when I realised this but it felt significant. As I marvelled at yet another Sandy connection, I felt something hit my leg. It was bird poop!!! The miracle of this is that it only hit my leg. It landed between the MEMORY STICK and the laptop. Neither was soiled, only my poor leg. Yep… just her kind of humour!

And so, as I conclude this story of my lovely Sandy and our metaphysical and meteoric friendship, I made a mental note to play the Lottery! I think it's Sandy's signature on our final chapter of this particular book (to be continued) and her inimitable seal of approval.

I will continue to live out my experience of this lifetime safe in the knowledge that when my time comes, and my mortal coil is shuffled off, it will be to the tune of *Take it Easy*. Sandy will be waiting in the sunlight with open arms, a giant sunflower in her hair, a glass of Margarita in one hand and an owl brooch in the other and the strains of *Daydream Believer* playing in the background. I would like everyone to drink Margaritas and toast my return to my Source and to my beloved friend and soul mate. I want them to know that I will be floating in pure bliss, catching up with all the news and no doubt practising the latest Jive techniques on a sparkling white beach with the crystal surf washing gently onto the shore.

And from there, our next chapter will begin…

*Jay Atkinson*
31st May 2010

www.solomonspeaks.org

# *About the Author*

Jay lives in a 1930's cottage in the middle of North Wales with her wonderful husband, Kim. Kim is a Master Chimney Sweep. Jay has three starbright offspring – now grown and flown - Jamie, Kate and Anna, all of whom she loves passionately.

She was born in the spring of 1956 in Cleethorpes, Lincolnshire to a beautiful mother and very handsome father and over her life has lived in Lincolnshire, Yorkshire, Northumberland and, for a very brief period, the South Pacific!

Jay has siblings and step-siblings who are scattered across the globe as far as Mallorca and Australia, but remains close to her sister, Gina and her brother Dean, both of whom still live in England with their families.

Jay is a natural medium/psychic and realised her ability when she began writing more seriously at the age of 15. When she was 18, she met a spiritual healer, who ran a healing sanctuary in Waltham, Lincolnshire. This lovely lady recognised Jay's talent as a gifted channeller (as they were called then) although it would be some years before this gift was utilised more fully.

In 1974, Jay worked as a receptionist for a prestige motor dealership. Her employer decided to enter her into the prestigious Miss Motor Show beauty contest at Earl's Court in London. She won. After a year of bright lights and glamour, Jay decided that it wasn't the path for her and began an inner journey instead.

She now devotes her life to her work as an interpreter of Source Energy, through her writing, her personal energy readings and her seminars and workshops. You can find out more about her and her work at her website: www.solomonspeaks.org

Lightning Source UK Ltd.
Milton Keynes UK
29 July 2010
157577UK00002B/1/P